Learning Employment Readiness Skills

How to re-enter today's competitive workforce

Your hands-on guide for achieving a
Meaningful employment conclusion

STEVE BRENNAN

BALBOA.
PRESS

A DIVISION OF HAY HOUSE

Balboa Press books may be ordered through booksellers or by contacting:

Balboa Press
A Division of Hay House
1663 Liberty Drive
Bloomington, IN 47403
www.balboapress.com
1-(877) 407-4847

Because of the dynamic nature of the Internet, any web addresses or links contained in this book may have changed since publication and may no longer be valid. The views expressed in this work are solely those of the author and do not necessarily reflect the views of the publisher, and the publisher hereby disclaims any responsibility for them.

The author of this book does not dispense medical advice or prescribe the use of any technique as a form of treatment for physical, emotional, or medical problems without the advice of a physician, either directly or indirectly. The intent of the author is only to offer information of a general nature to help you in your quest for emotional and spiritual well-being. In the event you use any of the information in this book for yourself, which is your constitutional right, the author and the publisher assume no responsibility for your actions.

Any people depicted in stock imagery provided by Thinkstock are models, and such images are being used for illustrative purposes only.

Certain stock imagery © Thinkstock.

ISBN: 978-1-4525-8204-7 (sc)
ISBN: 978-1-4525-8205-4 (e)

Library of Congress Control Number: 2013916655

Printed in the United States of America.

Balboa Press rev. date: 9/30/2013

Table of Contents

Before anything else, preparation is the key to success

—Alexander Graham Bell

Introduction

If you are really serious about attaining meaningful employment then you have picked up the right book. In today's difficult employment market there are many factors that lead to why an individual is hired or is not. Many people may be selected for a phone or face to face interview, leave feeling great but do not receive an employment offer.

People who have just graduated and are entering the workforce for the first time, those re-entering the workforce after being off for an extended period of time, individuals seeking to advance or change careers, and our returning veterans who have been trained in many disciplines which all have terrific transferable skills and may benefit from this material.

The information contained in this workbook will equip candidates with a set of skills which will assist them to stand out from other employment applicants. It will educate people to effectively search for employment, prepare to interview exceptionally, and supply them the confidence to achieve their desired result and land that new job.

I've been a Sr. Manager in fortune 500 corporations, and have had the express privilege & opportunity to interview countless personnel either by phone or in person, and have hired many individuals in varying employment skill sets.

During my 30 + years of tenure in these organizations I've developed & educated numerous employees utilizing various training modules, some of which include; Business Plan Development, Improving Time Management Skills, & Using Technology Effectively.

No matter how great your resume, interviewing skills, and preparation, the key to your long-term success will lie in your efforts. This book will provide you help in these specific areas.

Competition in the employment arena is fierce. Businesses have a wide range of applicants to choose from. People who once were the cream of the crop now find themselves competing with new graduates, with high academic credentials, and many individuals who possess more experience than once was available in the business community.

I would suggest you get out your highlighter because this book is packed with useable content.

In subsection 3.1.d for example, I review how to use "Word Pictures" or **SAR (Situation, Action, Result)** which will enable you to answer questions where experiential knowledge alone may not have the impact your interviewer is really seeking. This exercise helps separate you from the pack. One of the clients I tutored who successfully gained meaningful employment commented, "Throughout this book I found small bite-size consumables of content that gave me "Ah ha" moments.

But before you begin digesting this data let me reveal a little bit about myself. Every one of us faces challenges and setbacks. I was not immune to these.

At 17 years young, I was a high school dropout living in the back seat of a 1963 Dodge station wagon that my friend owned.

I knew I needed to find a job fast. Although I did have some experience as a young man doing the odd young man jobs, i.e. mowing and watering lawns, ironing, and even selling pot holders made by the blind. None of this terrific experiential knowledge qualified me for a "Regular Full Time Job." To top it all off my friend was moving, and I lost my fine station wagon abode.

I soon found out this getting a job idea was not an easy task. I applied everywhere. No one would even interview me. I was frustrated, hungry, tired, had no work, no place to live, and was not willing to go back home. I became desperate and I fell to my knees and prayed for a miracle.

I spent that night in the local park, and when the next day dawned, I felt something stirring inside of me. Today was the day I would get a job. I couldn't put my finger on it then, but I knew something was missing in my life. What I really needed all along was hope & the belief everything was going to be okay *(the miracle)*.

My first full time job was with a local tire company. I mustered up as much courage as humanly possible and marched right into the owner's office. Pat P. was a bigger than life Italian man from the old country he had a big mustache, hearty boisterous laugh and a robust profile to match.

I proceeded to tell him my situation and that I needed a job, I went on and said, "I'll work for you one week for free. However, after that week if I do everything you want as you instruct you'll have to hire me full time." After that week *I got the job!*

My story may be somewhat different or maybe similar to yours, I knew I needed to get an education, to further my career aspirations.

I'm also keenly aware that every journey begins with the first step. At the beginning of my passage from a person with little confidence in himself or marketable employment skills & abilities I did have one thing going for me. I believed everything I could do was possible with the help of God.

That was more than 47 years ago, and I've been employed since then but not in the same job, company, or skill set. What I gained in those 47 years has been invaluable and no less than miraculous. I learned how to gain and maintain successful meaningful employment. I earned an undergrad, BS in Business and MBA Degrees. And through it all I have an abiding faith in God, and continually trust and lean on Him first in all situations.

You may be saying, "Well, isn't that nice, but you really don't understand what I'm really up against," and that is probably true. However, it hasn't always been clear sailing, for me either. Yep, no roses and singing cherubs here. I've experienced financial, employment, and medical challenges. I've been let go from 4 jobs, could only afford to live in a 250 square foot one room apartment, and spaghetti O's was a main course meal. As a boy I was diagnosed with (CKD) Chronic Kidney Disorder.

After several operations including the removal of my left kidney my condition was stabilized. Over the next 25 years things appeared to be going smooth and my career was progressing. Then at age 54 after running my second ½ marathon I was diagnosed with a fast growing stage 4 cancer that metastasized to a lymph node. The doctors took aggressive action and prescribed chemotherapy and radiation treatment.

However, the chemo drugs took their toll on my one remaining kidney. I began dialysis 3 days a week and continued to travel for work full time, while waiting for a transplant.

Then another miracle happened. My beautiful spouse of 30 years was a match. How good is God? I received my new kidney which we call the *"Pretty Kidney."* By the way we are both doing great!

My life today is terrific. I've recently retired from my managerial assignment and will be teaching the material in this workbook at a local college, and conducting individual pre-employment mentoring & tutoring sessions.

One thing is for sure we will have tough periods in our life. It's not if they come, but when. I trust each of you will achieve your desired employment aspirations and can create the life you now can only dream of.

I'm convinced that everyone can succeed when they believe they can and put forth the effort required. Remember what Henry Ford said, "Whether you think you can, or you think you can't you're right."

Believe in your new found knowledge. It will benefit you and provide you with steadfast persistence. Have confidence in and know that God is with you.

"Congratulations!—
You're on Your Way to your New Career"

Is Applying For a Job Getting More Difficult?

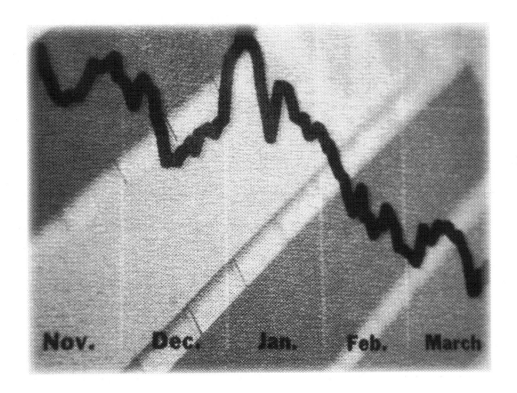

Department of Labor (DOL) report indicating that total nonfarm employment increased in May 2013 by 175,000 this was greeted with a collective sigh of modest relief. Unfortunately the June 11, 2013 DOL JOTLs (Job Openings and Labor Turnover) report of open jobs forecasts a summer of renewed hand-wringing.

There was a nice pickup in open jobs in February to almost 4mm resulting decent employment increases in April (+149K) and May (+175K). The Q1 flattening of total open jobs however is likely to be felt in the summer months since there's a lag of about 2-3 months after a job is posted before it's filled. So if a job-seeker is expecting to get a job by applying to a job posting, things will get more difficult. Source: USA Today June 19, 2013

Your Self-Assessment is first

- ➤ Define and understand your skills and interests
- ➤ Understand your strengths and qualifications
- ➤ List your short-term and long-term goals
- ➤ What type of work environments would you prefer?
- ➤ What other work values are important to you?

It's Time to reflect on these important issues

Goals & Expectations

- ➢ There *are* jobs out there but competition is keen for most of them
- ➢ In today's marketplace the average job search takes 4-6 months
- ➢ When you can clearly picture the type of job you want, you are more likely to be successful
- ➢ Remember that looking for a job is a job in itself!

Who is in your Network?

Every Person You Contact!

- ✓ Family
- ✓ Friend
- ✓ Co-worker
- ✓ Professors, staff
- ✓ Acquaintances

Some questions to ask your network

➤ "Who do you know that might have an opening for a person with my skills?" If no, then,
➤ "Is there anyone *else* who might know of someone who would?"
➤ "Do you know someone who knows lots of people?"

Specific Job Search Activities—Web-sites to visit

www.acinet.org/acinet/ or www.bls.gov/ooh/

Construct a daily routine for each day of the week, for example:

- ✓ New contacts/applications—Mornings
- ✓ Employer research—Mornings
- ✓ Networking—Afternoons
- ✓ Follow-ups—Afternoons
- ✓ Relaxation

Always maintain a solid method

- ➤ Conduct an organized search, keeping track of applications sent, follow-ups and interview dates.
- ➤ Convey positive energy.
- ➤ Always be courteous and gracious to everyone and don't forget the power of the **"thank you."**

What are responsibilities as the *Job Seeker?*

✓ Provide prepared accurate information about yourself on resumes and job applications.
✓ Show up on time for all scheduled interviews.
✓ Interview genuinely, and interview only for jobs you are truly interested in.
✓ Communicate your acceptance or refusal of a job offer as promptly as possible.
✓ Accept a job offer in good faith.
✓ Claim fair reimbursement if an employer agreed to reimburse you for costs incurred during your recruitment.

Reasons some job seekers get stuck—

- ➤ Not understanding that finding a job is a job itself.
- ➤ Lack of a system for finding work.
- ➤ Do not have a clear realistic view of the market and how their skills transfer.
- ➤ Don't recognize there is emotional stress seeking a job.
- ➤ Don't identify that 'getting the interview' is absolutely vital.
- ➤ Don't prepare well for interviews.
- ➤ Don't sell themselves in interviews.
- ➤ Interview with the attitude of "what can you do for me?"
- ➤ Refuse to consider a range of job possibilities.

Assess your job search activities

- ✓ Be willing to change job search tactics if something isn't working.
- ✓ Talk to successful job hunters and find out what techniques worked for them.
- ✓ Career counselors can help. Appraise them of your activities and listen to their advice.

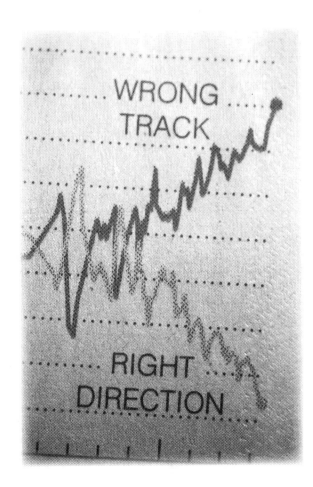

Physically take care of yourself

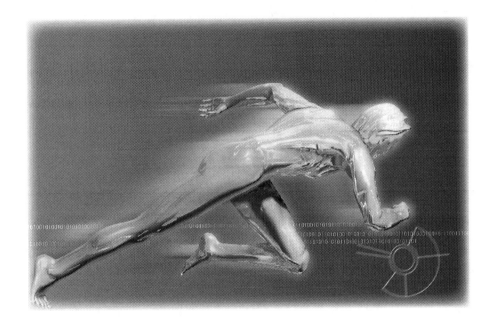

- ➤ Job searching can be demanding and frustrating. Make sure to get support.
- ➤ Involve your family and friends in your job search.
- ➤ Inform them of the seriousness of this project, and ask for their help and understanding.
- ➤ Remember your support group—don't be afraid to seek them out.
- ➤ Don't take rejection personally.
- ➤ Focus on the things you **can** control—your attitude, diet, exercise schedule, focus and organization.

➤ Section 1.1 Self-Assessment

What are your Skills, Interests, & Aspirations?

Definition of a Skill—An ability coming from ones knowledge, practical aptitude, or expertise. An ability to carry-out complex activities or job functions. These may include cognitive skills, technical skills, and interpersonal skills. To do something well.

I'm sure all of us at one time or another have worked at something that has given us great pride. It seems as though when we are engaged in this type of activity we do not feel as though we are laboring at all. We actually feel more alive. This sort of work seems natural, fun, exciting. Now ask yourself, this question, "What if I could do

_____ *"YOU FILL IN THE BLANK"* and make money too?"

Within us lie these three important attributes: Sincere Interest, Skills, and Aspirations. We need to identify yours.

It's like hitting a golf ball perfectly, making a cake that is out of this world, nailing the final, etc. Sometimes called; "Hitting the Sweet Spot." This is where our natural interests, skills, and aspirations collide.

1. Your Significant Skills

Identify your natural God given gifts and talents. Do you have a talent for woodworking or a terrific mechanical aptitude? Are you compassionate? Is nursing something that would excite you, or being a social worker? Inside all of us are talents, gifts, and skills.

Review what you know and have learned or could easily learn. The talents, gifts, and skills you have are a great source to begin looking at employment situations and where you most likely would be able to excel and thrive.

Of course, our talents, gifts, and skills are just a small part of what is necessary to succeed. However, when you combine them with your sincere interest you most certainly will open the right door for that new opportunity.

2. Your Sincere Interests

What do you dream of? When engaged in conversation what do you like to talk about? If money didn't matter what would you like to do? A sincere interest may produce monetary outcomes. What we love to do really energizes us. For example, woodworking, tinkering with an old car, baking, quilting, making jewelry, playing chess, fishing, hunting, etc. What do you enjoy reading about? What are your favorite subjects?

If you ended up in your current assignment by circumstance and are doing well, how much better can you perform in a position that you are sincerely interested in? We all want to feel good about ourselves and live happily.

I recognize each of us has a dependence on money. It's been said. "There is nothing that replaces money where money is used." Over the years, I've witnessed first-hand people going to work and performing exceptionally, but were they as happy as they could have been? Most likely, some yes, & some no.

I experienced this myself early on while working in a plastics factory. I went to work and did what was expected of me because I had obligations and needed the money. However, I was not very happy or being nourished. How about you?

Nothing came easy. It took time, commitment, and persistence. Attempting greatness without a sincere interest is like trying to make bread and leaving out the yeast. All extraordinary triumphs are made possible through your sincere interest.

3. Your "Aspiration Quotient"

Definition of Aspiration Quotient—An aspiration quotient is a collection of your skills, interests, desires, dreams, hopes, and yearnings. When we effectively combine these components together with an unswerving belief in ourselves and faith in God we have the formula.

We all want to achieve and be at the top of our game. This is not just in the employment world. Every boy dreams of going to the moon, hitting the winning home run, & making a jump shot at the buzzer to win the state basketball championship. And yes, let's not forget the girls.

What little girl hasn't wanted to be a winning athlete, class president, prom queen, or a great teacher?

Unfortunately this does not happen for many us. All too often we are average and really have to work at making our dreams come true. Therefore, it is crucial to identify your aspirations.

Good luck might happen right? Remember if we want opportunity we need to go and get it. There is no such this as "Good Luck." Luck is where opportunity meets preparedness.

My greatest aspiration came about unexpectedly, I was in the right place at the right time. However, prior to that serendipitous moment, I networked, I studied, I attended conferences, and most importantly, I was prepared. When we get in the game and create more activity for ourselves to meet and network with other people we will naturally improve our "Aspiration Quotient."

When we continue putting in the effort to improve our talents, gifts, and skills we will see our career aspirations come to fruition.

Subsection 1.1.a What do you consider are your strengths & qualifications?

Make a detailed list of all the training and qualifications that you have gained.

Academic, OTJ training, seminars, all of your abilities are a terrific asset that can help you when applying for jobs.

> ➤ List as many as you can & why they will help you & a prospective organization

Subsection 1.1.b What are your short-term & long-term goals?

Subsection 1.1.c What type of work environments do you prefer?

Office, Outdoors, Travel—Explain your reasons

Subsection 1.1.d What other work values are important to you?

> ➤ i.e. Non-competitive, friendly, inspiring—Explain your reasons

➤ **Section 2.1** Assess your employment skills

- *This is an important section—please take time completing*

Subsection 2.1.a Establishing career goals

- A concrete and attainable goal list is your first step in career development

Subsection 2.1.b SMART GOAL Template

- Use the SMART GOAL template

SMART GOALS—TEMPLATE

SMART goals help improve achievement and success. A SMART goal clarifies exactly what is expected and the measures used to determine if the goal is achieved and successfully completed.

A SMART goal is:

Specific (and strategic): Linked to position summary, departmental goals/mission, and/or overall goals and strategic plans. Answers the question—Who? and What?

Measurable: The success toward meeting the goal can be measured. Answers the question—How?

Attainable: Goals are realistic and can be achieved in a specific amount of time and are reasonable.

Relevant (results oriented): The goals are aligned with current tasks and projects and focus in one defined area; include the expected result.

Time framed: Goals have a clearly defined time-frame including a target or deadline date.

Examples:

Not a SMART goal:

- Employee will improve their writing skills.

Does not identify a measurement or time frame, nor identify why the improvement is needed or how it will be used.

SMART goal:

- The Department has identified a goal to improve communications with administrative staff by implementing an internal departmental newsletter. Elaine will complete a business writing course by January 2010 and will publish the first monthly newsletter by March 2010. Elaine will gather input and/or articles from others in the department and draft the newsletter for supervisor review, and when approved by supervisor, distribute the newsletter to staff by the 15th of each month.

SMART Goal Planning Form

Specific—WHO? WHAT?

Measurement/Assessment—HOW?

Attainable/Achieve—REASONABLE?

Relevant—EXPECTED RESULT?

By

Timed—WHEN?

Subsection 2.1.c *http://skillcow.com/skilltest*

- Skill assessment exercise quiz

Subsection 2.1.d *http://www.cao.ac.za/Quiz.aspx*

- Your work personality Quiz

➢ **Section 3.1** Pre-Employment Development Exercises

Subsection 3.1.a Understanding your transferrable skills

Subsection 3.1.b & c—*Copy these and insert into your browser*

http://www.centerstagegroup.com/public/Transferable_Skills_Inventory_People.htm
http://www.quibblo.com/quiz/aw8npyx/DISC-Personality-Style

Subsection 3.1.d Assets & Industry & Career Options

Make a List of your Tangible & Intangible—Examples Below

Assets:

Industry and Career Options

National / International Sales Account Manager

Vice President—Sales / Operations

TANGIBLE
Management
International Experience
Strategic Planning
Business Planning
Reorganization
Negotiation Procurement
Materials Inventory
Management Vendor Relations
Staff Management Finance

Budgeting
Cost Accounting
Accounts Receivable / Credit Management Operational Management
Workflow Analysis External/Internal Customer Service Outsourcing
ISO-9000
QS-9000
Logistics P&L
Sales & Marketing
New product development New Account Development Promotions
Sales Management—Commercial/Retail OEM
Publicity Events Mass Merchandizing
Aftermarket Automotive
Commercial Vehicles
International experience
Marketing Plans Training
Dealer Networks

INTANGIBLE
Contract Negotiations
Achievement Oriented
Adaptable Enthusiastic
Planner Coach
Conscientiousness Determined
Disciplined Reliable
Thoughtful Flexible
Open-Minded
Quality Conscious Focused
Leader Honest Logical
Objective

Source: S Brennan

Subsection 3.1.e Word Strength Descriptors

Word Strength Descriptors you develop are ways to help you to describe yourself & strengths. There could be times when you are quizzed about a particular issue, skill, or given situation. These word descriptors are to help provide you with quick responses that you can then follow-up with in sentence form. This is a helpful exercise to keep individuals from stumbling during a phone or in person interview.

Steve Brennan

Write 10 Word Strength Descriptor Sentences, without using your word in the sentence. (see examples below)

Word Strength Descriptions/Sentences

1. Achiever
When presented with an assignment, directive, objective, or deadline, I'm known to be a person who can be counted on to accomplishing them.

2. Demanding
I attack situations that require immediate action like a surgeon, and I expect 100% dedication of myself and others on the team to carry through.

3. Effective
I provide meaningful and appropriate contributions when given a directive or assignment. I assure measurable results on a consistent basis.

4. Flexible
I respond creatively and positively to requirements for changed approaches, roles, behaviors and skills generated by changing business conditions.

Subsection 3.1.f S.A.R.

> ➢ Write a minimum of 4 S.A.R.'s examples whereby you accomplished or had successes in various assignments that you were directly responsible for.

Sometimes in the interview process we are asked a question designed to help the interviewer better understand a process or assignment that is related to the position that you're applying for.

By answering with a S.A.R. it allows individuals to use *"Word Pictures"* to provide a concrete example to their interviewer. Try using the following S.A.R.s example instead.

Interview question.

Have you ever implemented a project? Was it successful? Rather than answering. "Yes I've implemented many in my career and my success in doing so was terrific."

SARS Example Document

Situation:

Our customers purchased approximately $10 million in compression fittings from us annually for a variety of products. These fittings were very reliable yet labor intensive during the installation process.

Action:

I introduced a new PTC (Push to Connect) fitting that would reduce time and labor cost. However, the piece part price was more expensive.

Result:

Through a sequence of meetings with the engineering, materials and the purchasing departments I recommended a cross functional team be assembled to do a beta test on selected brake valves to evaluate the efficiency of these fittings. The end result was these fitting were adopted with improved productivity. The departments saved time; and subsequently we increased our sales and gross profit margin within that business unit.

Source: S Brennan

➢ Section 4.1 The Resume

Many of you may have an excellent resume especially for the assignment and career that you've chosen. However, if you are now looking to change to a new career you should consider utilizing more than one resume. This is essential when applying for positions or postings on electronic and social media job boards. Style is important. Additionally, the old adage of a one page resume is not accurate.

Many seasoned professionals that have had successful career tracks should expound on their achievements and successes. In that case their resume could be 2 – 5 pages.

Below are some examples that you could use and word smith to fit your own career objectives.

Operations Management Executive Resume Sample

Functional Resume Sample

George Goodman

123 N. First Street ~ Williamsburg, Virginia 23081

804-123-5555, <u>Ggoodman@thebest.net</u>

<u>SUMMARY OF QUALIFICATIONS</u>

Accomplished, seasoned Professional with proven success in operations management to achieve the organizational mission. Superior communication skills, easily interacts with executives, regulatory agencies, clients, vendors, and staff. Technically proficient in spreadsheets, word processing, graphics, & accounting software. Member AICPA.

PROFESSIONAL EXPERIENCE

<u>Operations Management</u>

- Oversee all operational matters for a contract electronic manufacturing plant, in particular management development and strategic planning.
- Spearheaded effort for ISO 9001 certification.
- Secured financing for turnkey manufacturing; implemented new methods to track and improve profitability.

<u>Financial Administration</u>

- Supervised accounting staff with direct oversight of all accounting, payroll, & banking activities.
- Acquired lines of credit and initiated effective collection processes.
- Implemented GAAP-compliant financials and tax-planning strategies.

<u>Compliance & Training</u>

- Administered all areas of Agency compliance.
- Established periodic compliance audits & reviews; performed daily compliance supervision.

- Organized and conducted full operations training, from investments & insurance to financial & tax planning; directed client relations.

WORK HISTORY

ELECTRONICS EDGE, INC., Williamsburg, Virginia 1999-Present
Chief Operating Officer

FINANCE TEAM, INC., Baltimore, Maryland 1993-1999
Director of Compliance & Training (1996-1999)

SPHERE ROBOTICS, Washington, D.C. 1985-1993
Subcontract Administrator (1992-1993)

EDUCATION

GEORGETOWN UNIVERSITY, Washington, D.C.
Master of Business Administration, Financial Management Emphasis, 1987

STANFORD UNIVERSITY, Stanford, California
Bachelor of Science in Accounting, Minor in Business, 1979

Intermediary Business Analyst Resume Sample

Marsha Owens, MBA

5622 Grand Drive, Santa Fe, New Mexico 87101

505-555-1212, Owen2@Owen.net

QUALIFICATIONS

Business Analyst with superior analytical skills applied to contract negotiations, business processes, data collection and management for major health providers, including Health First. Consistently promoted to positions of increased responsibility, advancing three times within a one-year period. Excellent communicator with fluency in English and Spanish. Proven leadership in training employees and conducting formal presentations to all levels of management. Outstanding academic credentials in business, international management, and analytical finance.

SELECTED ACCOMPLISHMENTS

- Completed contracting for 6,000+ providers within 6 months for CHAMPUS contract.
- Improved production 20% through the establishment of department production standards.
- Launched marketing department for the State of New Mexico.

PROFESSIONAL EXPERIENCE

Financial & Business Analysis

- Performed complex analyses for system-wide negotiations, projections, and line-of-business reviews in addition to analysis of population distribution, claim/utilization, and cost.
- Identified, collected, and organized data from multiple sources for input into monthly, quarterly, annual, and ad hoc reports provided to contracting/finance departments and senior management.
- Designed and implemented database applications used in contract rate and risk management analysis as well as the identification and correction of date errors and discrepancies.

Management & Supervision

- Analyzed, interpreted, and resolved claims with authorization for payments up to $75,000.
- Directed activities of 40 claims analysts at a large project site.
- Interacted daily with enrolment, claims, utilization/quality management, and customer service to resolve provider issues.

EMPLOYMENT HISTORY

HEALTH FIRST, Albuquerque, New Mexico, 1997-2003
Manager, Contract Analysis/Senior Financial Analyst

FEDERAL HEALTH SERVICES, Albuquerque, New Mexico, 1994-1997
Manager, Provider Relations

CROSS HEALTH CARE, Albuquerque, New Mexico, 1993-1994
Risk Analyst

GROUP SERVICES, Albuquerque, New Mexico, 1990-1993
Senior Claims Analyst/Project Manager

EDUCATION

GRADUATE SCHOOL OF BUSINESS, Albuquerque, New Mexico
Master of Business Administration, 1992

NEW WEST UNIVERSITY, Albuquerque, New Mexico
Bachelor of Arts in Business, 1989

Source: Previously posted as a free example,—by http://www.ResumeEdge.com a leading provider of resume editing and writing, cover letters, and LinkedIn profiles. The name, address, phone, & email, have been changed

Hybrid Resume Sample 1 (Marketing Executive)

A Hybrid resume is a combination of reverse chronological and functional resumes.

Sally Majors

1543 Little Park Drive ~ New York, New York 10001

212.555.1212, Thebest1@purpose.com

MARKETING EXECUTIVE

Product Launches ~ Overseas Partnerships ~ Presentations

Accomplished, multilingual Professional consistently recognized for achievement and performance in the fuel industry. Innovative and successful in mining new sales territories and establishing business alliances, including the recent partnership with M.IM Oil in Korea. Proven leader with special capabilities in building teams, strategizing, and implementing workable marketing plans employing television, radio, Internet, and print media. Fluent in English, Korean, Japanese, and French.

BUSINESS SKILLS

Marketing

- Launch gasoline exports in conjunction with new production plant start-up; target overseas markets.
- Initiate sales of ULS, an environmentally-friendly new product launched in the European market.
- Establish joint venture partnerships in Europe and Far East; implement marketing for aviation fuel and asphalt as a value-added commodity.

Market Planning

- Analyze regional import / export economies and the interregional oil markets.
- Participate in contact negotiations for strategic alliances with a major European and Asian concurs.
- Achieved $25 million in revenue by developing offshore storage programs that fulfilled seasonal market trends in the region.

Product Planning

- Optimize production mode by selecting appropriate refinery; research product specification revisions by country.
- Propose and participate in the Plant Operation Committee, a team effort between production and sales.

PROFESSIONAL EXPERIENCE

TTR CORPORATION, New York, New York 1993-Present
Vice President, Overseas Business Division

- Promoted to position in March 1996; selected as one of the three employees to attend an MBA course in 2003.
- Named Employee of the Year in 1996 based on professional achievements.

FUEL INDUSTRY OF AMERICA, New York, New York 1989-1992
Manager of Marketing

- Provided analysis on fuel industry, drafting report for the White House.
- Awarded the Honor Prize in 1992 based on performance evaluations of oil producers.

EDUCATION

UNIVERSITY OF NEW YORK, New York, New York
Bachelor of Arts in Communications, 1988

Hybrid Resume Sample 2 (Athletic Director)

Bob Davis

378 Landon Way ~ Las Vegas, Nevada 89128
702-555-1212, Davis 2@Pro.com

ATHLETIC DIRECTOR COACH ADMINISTRATOR TEACHER

Articulate, student-focused individual with proven expertise in motivating youth to achieve goals, while also prioritizing and strategizing for winning school athletic programs. Holds students, parents, and staff in high esteem, and interacts with the greatest degree of professionalism and personal integrity. Background includes leadership in the educational field and in business. Dedicated to student and staff development. Proficient with athletic scheduling software.

ATHLETICS EXPERIENCE

NEVADA PRIVATE BOYS SCHOOL, Las Vegas, Nevada 2001-Present
Athletic Director, Boys Varsity Basketball Coach

- Exceeded Athletic Association standards by reorganizing Athletic Department.
- Created new policies and procedures and rewrote Athletic Handbook.

ATHLETIC CONFERENCES, Las Vegas, Nevada 2001-Present
President and Member

- Functions Acting President of Nevada Athletic Conference (NAC).
- Participate in National Interscholastic Athletic Administrators Association (NIAAA) and Nevada State Interscholastic Athletic Administrators Association (NSIAAA). Attend NIAAA leadership classes.

HIGH SCHOOL ATHLETICS, Las Vegas, Nevada 1999-2001
Junior Varsity Basketball Coach (2000-2001), Assistant Basketball Coach (1999-2000)

- Coached Junior Varsity team and assisted Varsity coach at Nevada Private Boys School.
- Assisted Varsity and Junior Varsity Basketball teams in Division 1 at Desert High School.

Steve Brennan

EDUCATIONAL EXPERIENCE

NEVADA PRIVATE BOYS SCHOOL, Las Vegas, Nevada 2001-Present
Assistant Principal, Dean of Students, Teacher

- Assist Principal daily with duties, and handle most disciplinary matters.
- Instruct students in algebra, physical education, and computer science.
- Improved several school policies and procedures, and revised student handbook.

NEVADA PRIVATE GRADE SCHOOL, Las Vegas, Nevada 2000-2001
Honors Algebra Teacher

BUSINESS EXPERIENCE

Private Accountant, Trammel Bookkeeping Company, Las Vegas, Nevada (1999-2001)
Accounting Analyst, Statewide Data Systems, Las Vegas, Nevada (1995-1999)
Corporate Accountant, Bryant Division, Inc., Las Vegas, Nevada (1993-1995)

EDUCATION

CALIFORNIA STATE UNIVERSITY, Fullerton, California
Bachelor of Science in Business Administration, Finance, 1993

Hybrid Resume Sample 3 (Sales Professional)

Robert Knowledge

672 Marble Hill ~ Denver, Colorado 80127

303-555-1212, Knowledgebase@wired.com

SALES PROFESSIONAL

Client Relations ~ Negotiations ~ Inside & Outside Sales

Dynamic and results-oriented with a successful track record in the industrial sales industry and a desire to move into pharmaceutical sales. Articulate and persuasive in dealing with all levels of management, peers, staff, and a diverse clientele. Consistently meets and exceeds corporate sales goals, while also mentoring staff to improve customer satisfaction. Special abilities in attention to detail, decision-making, organization, and marketing plans. Willing to travel.

CAREER ACCOMPLISHMENTS TRENT CORPORATION

Outside Sales

- In six months achieved an 80% overall sales increase in accounts excluding the Mohawk-Karastan national contract that Trent Corporation previously lost, with this account representing 59% of the territory's revenue.
- Retained 50% of Mohawk-Karastan business through creative marketing plans.
- Selected to attend and successfully completed companies prestigious outside sales management trainee program.

Inside Sales

- Chosen to manage VIP clients, including APV Baker and E.I DuPont representing annual revenues of $2 million.
- Led inside sales staff in monthly gross profit and total sales.
- Increased total monthly gross profit by 249% in seven months.

PROFESSIONAL EXPERIENCE

TRENT CORPORATION, Denver, Colorado 1999-Present
Sales Professional, Outside Sales (2001-Present)
Inside Sales (2000-Present); Corporate Trainee (1999-2000)

- Recognized by company for outstanding sales service and consistent leadership in reaching company goals.
- Chosen to be a corporate trainee.
- Taught Introduction to Distribution Class to branch employees.
- Completed training in all phases of business, including operations, product lines, sales, and distribution.
- Traveled to numerous branches to assist with sales-related issues.
- Marketed territory for new sales representative; developed improvements to cold-calling technique.
- Mined sales opportunities by conducting on-site surveys with consumers.

Additional Experience as a Collections Manager and Collector for Industrial Acceptance Corporation in Denver, Colorado.

EDUCATION

COLORADO CITY COLLEGE, Denver, Colorado
Bachelor of Arts in Psychology, English Minor, 1996

Source: Previously posted as a free example,—by http://www.ResumeEdge.com a leading provider of resume editing and writing, cover letters, and LinkedIn profiles. The name, address, phone, & email, have been changed

Foreman Resume Sample
Functional Resume Example

Dwayne Leonard

922 Wild Curve Circle ~ Providence, Rhode Island 02901 USA
401-523-1234, DL2@myworld.com

FOREMAN

Carpentry ~ General Construction ~ Quality Control Management ~ Project Management Certificate

Results-oriented skilled Professional with solid supervisory background and experience working on projects in the United States and overseas. Background includes completing assignments in challenging environments, including areas of civil unrest, those with semi-skilled labor, and during supply shortages. Private sector experience in industrial/commercial and large, multi-unit residential projects; military experience includes seismic retrofits, modernization, and resident improvements. Technically proficient with PCs and peripherals. Physically fit to meet the demands of construction. Willing to relocate and free to travel; single with no dependents; holds a valid US Passport.

CAREER ACCOMPLISHMENTS

- Served as the Assistant Quality Control Manager on a $14 million US Navy modernization project.
- Trained and experienced in industrial hygiene/safety, security, and as an Emergency Med Tech/ Firefighter/ Hazmat Response Technician.
- Hold a Class A Commercial Driver's License with T and X endorsements; possess clear driving record for well over ten years.
- Successfully worked with US citizens and foreign nationals; British West Indies indigenous workers; Bosnian governmental officials, Serb, Muslim, Croat, workers, and firefighters in Bosnia-Herzegovina; and Marshallese workers in The Republic of The Marshall Islands.
- Provided emergency response for Bosnian civilian population; liaised with local officials, UNPROFOR and UNHCR personnel.
- Possesses current First Aid and CPR certifications.

PROFESSIONAL EXPERIENCE

Construction (US)

- Reads and follows structural plans to lay out or check layout of sites and structures of varying sizes and functions.
- Laid out, formed, shored/poured foundations, structures, and flatwork.
- Framed with wood and metal, including structural steel members.
- Hung and finished drywall and related wall/ceiling systems.
- Performed exterior/interior finish carpentry that included door hanging and cabinet installation.
- Uses various instruments to check grade, line, and other measurements.
- Operates light to medium construction equipment.
- Experienced in driving trucks in OTR, construction, and oil/gas field operations.
- Provided safety, industrial hygiene, and emergency response at the Generation and Transmission Power Plant.

Construction (Overseas)

- Refurbished burned-out structure into United National Fire/EMS Station #1 in Sarajevo.
- Repaired a concrete roof structure that took an artillery hit in Sarajevo; prepared living quarters for Med Tech/ Firefighters.
- Worked on a challenging West Indies project with semi-skilled local labor and a shortage of supplies.

Source: Previously posted as a free example,—by http://www.ResumeEdge.com a leading provider of resume editing and writing, cover letters, and LinkedIn profiles. The name, address, phone, & email, have been changed

Thomas Claremont

124 West Miracle Mile DR

Gig Harbor, Washington 98335

Thomas 2@peoplenet.com—253.299.7272

SALES, BUSINESS DEVELOPMENT & GENERAL MANAGEMENT

Heavy-duty Industrial, Capital Equipment & Automotive Industries

---

Nationally recognized and award-winning Senior Executive with extensive experience, leading with forward thinking, vision, and strategy for success in sales, business development and general management, generating double-digit sales and profit growth in both domestic and international markets. Unique combination of knowledge in the automotive, capital equipment, and heavy-duty industrial markets blended with team leadership ensures quick grasp of market opportunities and ability to evangelize company vision. Highly skilled in business development, building market presence, and establishing profitable business practices. Interact cohesively with manufacturing, maintaining an understanding of manufacturing models and JIT. Compelling sense of business and work ethic with fearless drive. **MBA.**

New Business / Market Development	*Sales & Marketing Leadership*	*Multi-Site Operations Management*
New Product Development	*Cost Containment & Profit Growth*	*Dealer Networks*
Retail Operations Management	*Aftermarket Sales*	*Channel Sales & Distribution*
Branding, Promotions & PR	*Teambuilding & People Development*	*Budgeting & P&L*

Ranked #1 in Sales—Awarded "Manager of the Year"—for benchmarking innovative five-point process that propelled division ranked dead last in sales to first place in one year. Division generated $1 million in new revenue and won national award.

Global Market Development—Increased sales by 20% ($12 million) by penetrating international markets in Canada and Mexico. Directly responsible for new product development, leadership and direction.

Aggressive Turnaround—Reduced past due accounts 76% and returned retail outlet to profitable in one year by dramatically improving sales from an eight year loss and reducing operation expenses.

Skilled Negotiator—Successfully negotiated record-breaking national sales contract with Costco that resulted in $21 million in new account revenue.

Teambuilding—Achieved corporate objectives and individual goals by building teams that are motivated with strong complementary skill sets, training, and mentoring teams. Provided results-driven structure, and unified commitment, for a standard of excellence that inspired passion. Led with a "make it happen" winning attitude.

PROFESSIONAL EXPERIENCE

Ingersoll-Rand—2005—Retired

District Sales Manager

Accountable for all sales, budgets, and district P&L. Responsible to develop and implement all processes related to B2B and major account sales & action plans of Thermo King Refrigeration capital equipment. Consultative strategy with dealership owners & major account CEO's & CFO's on capital equipment purchase transactions. Consistently exceed corporate goals and objectives.

- Responsible for all sales & profit generating $50MM in district
- Continue to exceed annual revenue objective
- Develop revenue plans, implement forecasting methodologies, develop annual revenue and strategic planning process
- Member of the Team that Secured a Guaranteed Maintenance Contract for CR England Trucking &, H&R Transport. These comprised a 3 year Long Term Agreement (s) with recurring annual revenue in the millions

Ingersoll-Rand

District Parts Manager—2005-2006
Implemented action plans for dealership revenue improvement, conducted individual sales training, incentive promotions, & business planning process. Significantly increased dealer parts business. Developed sales strategies, select marketing programs to assist the growth of Thermo King Aftermarket Parts. Trained parts managers, which improved dealer profits.

- Created new competitive parts strategy & converted 10 new competitive accounts
- Signed first (PPA) Preferred Parts Alliance with C.R. England parts growth of $450K annual

- Achieved 112% to objective in 2005 with additional revenue growth of $8 Million
- Awarded District Parts Manager of the Year 2005

E-A-R Specialty Composites (2002 to 2005)

Industrial Account Manager

Western Region Account Executive of OEM sales to PACCAR and sales functions at Kenworth & Peterbilt manufacturing truck plants and divisions. Scope included budgeting, sales training, sales promotions, and business development.

- Maximized sales with effective leadership of three contract representative organizations with direct reports of 10 personnel in Canada, Arizona & California.
- Opened new distribution channel in Portland, Oregon that increased revenue in that market from $160,000 to $900,000.
- Participated in development of revenue plan, implementing forecasting methodologies, developing annual revenue and strategic planning process.
- Competitively positioned company with aggressive forward thinking in developing marketing strategy that coordinated sales and marketing, as well as created brand strategies focusing sales efforts in a key growth market segment.
- Led by example, promoting teamwork and information sharing with the goal of strengthening overall organization, motivating sales team to meet and exceed goals.

Country Green (2000 to 2001)

Contract Basis

Recruited to develop a business plan & to facilitate and improve sales and marketing functions, as well as provide sales training for 3 outside territory managers and inside account sales staff.

- Unprecedented sales volume achieved increasing sales 10% and improving overall gross margins 3% by developing extensive sales and marketing business plans and successfully implementing.
- Enhanced profit contributions by individual business units by evaluating and recommending pricing strategies.
- Negotiated with major suppliers that resulted in substantial material cost reductions.
- Drove performance improvement of three regional sales managers and six inside customer account representatives through training, motivation and mentoring.

PACCAR (1995 to 2000)

Fast track through several positions each with increasing responsibility within the division. Starting revenues from $50 million and 110 employees, to $160 million and 230 employees.

Aftermarket Sales & Marketing Manager (1999 to 2000)

Distinguished performance as OEM Sales and Business Development Manager led to promotion to Aftermarket Sales & Marketing Manager to handle Dynacraft's aftermarket sales department, expenses and budget, and mentor and manage seven regional sales managers.

- Significantly increased dealer parts business and program involvement with Dynacraft products, by developing a combined comprehensive operating business plan that included dealer sales planning and execution.
- Launched several new products and programs that contributed to achieving aftermarket sales goals resulting in driving up core business product sales for drive belts 25%, air conditioning parts 20% and Mexico total market sales 33%.
- Adept at communicating with staff to outline and assign duties, responsibilities, and scope of authority, as well as providing appropriate reports.
- Introduced strategies for Six Sigma cost reductions that optimized processes by creating diagnostic and reporting tools.

PACCAR

OEM Sales & Business Development Manager (1997 to 1999)

Direct management of all Dynacraft OEM sales and customer support activities. Accountable for expenses and budget of $1.1 million, direct reports16 employees.

- Identified, recommended and implemented new products through engineering, purchasing and materials management.
- Dramatically improved rolled yield throughput for the division (from $75 to $90 million) by outsourcing subassemblies at all Kenworth & Peterbilt plants worldwide.
- Expanded manufacturing opportunities for core Dynacraft products and supplier contacts.
- Consistently exceeded corporate goals and objectives by developing strategies and actions, and integrated goals within the organization and other departments.

- Liaised with production, materials, engineering, quality and senior manufacturing plant management for quality management functions of QS9000 and APQP process disciplines.

PACCAR

OEM Sales Manager (1995 to 1997)

Results driven global leadership of OEM sales throughout all Kenworth & Peterbilt manufacturing plants. Direct contact for plant personnel and corporate purchasing directors. Coordinated suppliers, JIT and delivery of product.

- Generated $12 million in new OEM revenue for Dynacraft at the Kenworth Mexico and Canadian manufacturing plants and improved sales to Kenworth Australia 15%.
- Accomplished corporate objectives by reviewing, recommending and procuring outsource production opportunities from truck manufacturing facilities to support JIT assembly plants.
- Delivered strong and sustainable gains by identifying and reviewing sales opportunities with Dynacraft management.
- Enhanced production by introducing process methodologies, introducing who, what, when and how benefits.
- Wrote documentation for ISO 9000 qualification for section 4.3.2 contract review that contributed to successfully passing ISO 9000 audit.

Dunlop Tire Corporation (1991 to 1994)

National Account Sales Manager

Spearheaded all national accounts for $500 million international tire manufacturer. Responsible for budgets, dealer sales, sales training, sales promotions, and business planning. Recognized for outstanding achievements, awarded **Western National Manager of the Year** 1991-1994 and **National Account Manager of the Year** 1992-1993.

- Identified and secured new National Account Fleets, being extremely proactive in advancing the sales of Dunlop truck tires. Grew revenues 110% with new account sales improving from $300,000 to $500,000 annually.
- Embraced a team approach while providing strong motivational leadership and commitment to excellence that resulted in increased efficiency and productivity; held meetings for continued product knowledge and training.

- Increased dealer sales involvement that in turn improved dealer profits by fostering better understanding of company vision and mission.
- Significantly improved market share and sales team productivity by developing and implementing new group sales structure.
- Effectively monitored progress toward objectives and report results on an ongoing basis, making regular adjustments as necessary.

EDUCATION

M.B.A., Regent / Barrington University (2001)
B.S. Business Administration, California Coast University (1993)
Ongoing Professional Development
Affiliation / Training Certification

FINANCE CHAIRMAN OF NON-PROFIT ORGANIZATION
FORMER MEMBER OF THE TMC (THE MAINTENANCE COUNCIL)
FORMER MEMBER BOARD OF DIRECTORS OPTIMIST INT'L
KARRASS EFFECTIVE NEGOTIATING SKILLS & DALE CARNEGIE NEGOTIATING SKILLS
ROOT CAUSE ANALYSIS / LEAN SIX SIGMA LEADERSHIP
BATTELLE INSTITUTE FOR MANAGERIAL LEADERSHIP
TEAM BUILDING EXERCISES—BOEING SPACE CENTER
TECHNICAL SALES TRAINING—COOPERS & LYBRAND

Source: Previously Published S. Brennan

Subsection 4.1.a Resume tips

A resume is a self-promotional document that makes the case for an interview. It normally accompanies a cover letter and presents your background in the most "objective" light possible. Your cover letter is your introduction to the employer and your resume is the document that "supports" that introduction. For instance, your cover letter may state that you have extensive experience in forensic accounting. Your resume is the document that will support that statement with more specifics.

Everything that you write in your resume has to serve a purpose. Screen out all the non-essentials. Once you have decided what information to include in your resume, you must think of the best way to present that information. How to phrase your work experience? What headings to use? What should you bold, if anything? What resume format to use?

Writing a resume is a lot of work, but if you break down the process in stages, it will look less insurmountable. The first step in writing a resume is to reflect. Don't rush to your computer yet. Answer these few basic questions:

- What are my strengths?
- What are my weaknesses?
- How to best present my strengths?
- What should I emphasize?
- How can I distinguish myself from other applicants?
- How can I convey to the employer that I am the best candidate for the job?

Once you know what to say, sit down and think of the best way to say it. Don't stop at the first draft, but work through many. When you are done with a final first draft, let it rest and come back on it a few hours or a day later. Read it out loud. If possible, ask trusted friends or family members for their feedback.

Remember that the main purpose of a resume is to get you an interview. Once you get that interview, no matter how impressive your resume looks compared to others, you will be put on an equal footing. From thereon, the decision to hire you or not will be based mainly on how you performed at the interview.

With that in mind, don't forget that a resume is a promotional tool, so don't be modest. At the same time, don't lie or exaggerate your skills if you cannot back them up. We hope that these resume tips will put you on the right path. Good luck!

Source S. Brennan/previously posted—Google Internet Public Domain

Subsection 4.1.b Questions to ask when writing your resume

Writing a resume can feel like one of the most challenging aspects of a job search. There's no doubt that writing this document requires a lot of introspection. But oftentimes, the challenge comes with a lack of true insight into your own career.

We spend a lot of time working on our jobs, but rarely give thought to the specific contributions we make to our employers in our roles. A good way to identify those contributions while providing insight into what information should be included in your resume is to ask yourself specific questions about your career.

1. What Are My Marketable Skill Sets?

As you create your resume, you want to think about the skills you bring to the table that would deem you to be a desirable candidate to a future employer. Take time to examine the skills you acquired with your previous employers. What were your primary contributions and how do these contributions help you to qualify for the role you want now?

2. How Would I Describe Myself in My Career?

As you examine your career as a whole, how would you describe yourself? Are you a natural leader? Do you love to initiate projects and see them developed and implemented? Are you the type of person who asks your manager how you can make contributions to enhance the company you work for? Take a look at the type of worker you are to help you remember top moments in your professional history when you truly made a difference. Also, try to recall instances when you were rewarded for your hard work so that you can add these details to your resume.

3. What Makes Me Stand Out From the Pack?

While you likely have a great deal of experience and highly attractive marketable skills, you are one of several qualified candidates competing for the same positions. What qualities do you bring to the table that make you stand out from the pack? Are you highly skilled in a software program that most people in your position are not? Think about what truly makes you a top choice for the position you want, and then add this information to your resume.

Once you've asked yourself these questions, you will have greater insight into what makes you the right person for the job you are interested in acquiring. Then you can use this insight to create an attractive resume that sells you as the perfect candidate for the job.

Source: Previously posted By: Jessica Holbrook Hernandez www.greatresumesfast.com

Subsection 4.1.c Three Ways to create a recession proof resume

It's no secret that a recession is one of the toughest times to find employment. With millions of workers looking for positions, your competition is incredibly steep. The good news is that job seeking during a recession doesn't mean you can't be hired. It does mean, however, that you will need to work to secure a job. A great way to increase your chances of being hired is by creating a recession-proof resume.

What is a Recession-Proof Resume?

A recession-proof resume is one that is able to get you hired under the toughest of economic conditions. With dozens—and sometimes even hundreds—of job seekers vying for the same position, it's pertinent that you find ways to make yourself stand out from the pack.

The recession-proof resume is able to accomplish this goal because it brings forward your strongest qualities as a professional in your field. It helps ensure you're able to find a quality job even when it seems no one is being hired, making it immune to the conditions of a recession.

3 Tips for Writing a Quality Recession-Proof Resume

So how can you create a resume that you believe will get you hired, even in the midst of a recession? Here are three tips to help you as you write:

1. **Think from the perspective of success:** It's easy for job seekers to simply jot down a general summary of their professional background, which doesn't give employers a good indication of how you can make a difference for them. So as you write, think about all of the successful moments of your career, then list very specific accomplishments that prove you can make the same progress with a new employer.

2. **Focus on keywords and phrases:** It's important to always remember that most employers utilize resume scanning software that helps them determine almost immediately how closely your background matches their qualification requirements. To give yourself a leg up on the competition, it's important to utilize job-specific keywords and phrases found in the job posting that show you are indeed a good match for the position.

3. **Prove you're specialty driven:** If you're applying for position as a human resources manager, for instance, it's important that you prove you're well trained in human resources. Take time to list your duties in action-oriented phrases, mention at least one major accomplishment per position, and be sure to highlight special training or programs you've been involved with that make you more qualified than other candidates.

Finding employment during tough economic times is not a simple task because so many qualified candidates are submitting their resumes at the same time. But don't let the steep competition deter you. Instead, step up your resume-writing creativity so that yours is so amazing that employers can't help but choose you for the position.

Source: Previously posted By: Jessica Holbrook Hernandez www.greatresumesfast.com

Subsection 4.1.d Four tips for making your resume a perfect match for an opening

When a hiring manager reviews your resume you want them to say, "Wow! That person sounds like the perfect fit for the job!" And then, of course, they call you for the interview! So how do you create a resume that communicates that you're exactly what they're looking for in a new employee? Below are four tips for creating a perfect-match resume.

1. Customization is critical

Remember, you always want to tweak your resume when you apply for a job. No two positions are exactly alike, and each employer is going to have different standards and requirements that are very important to them. Key in on those requirements, and be sure to incorporate them into your resume. You'll know what these requirements are by reviewing the job advertisement and noting special keywords throughout; or, in most cases, the employer will state **required skills** or **preferred qualifications.** You're a perfect match when you meet all of the required and preferred qualifications. Which leads me to my next point.

2. Required and preferred skills are essential

When reviewing the description for a job opening, be careful to note exactly what the employer lists as required and preferred. This is critical information. You want to make sure your resume communicates very clearly that you possess all of the **required** skills. This means you're capable of doing the job and performing the essential functions. Preferred qualifications are the employer's wish list of things they'd like to have in a new employee. They can live without them, but if you can prove you possess them, you just upped the ante for the other candidates being considered and are one step closer to positioning yourself as the ideal candidate.

3. Keywords are a must

Scan the opening for important keywords listed throughout. Chances are any recruiter or HR person is going to use these keywords when searching job boards for your resume. You want to make sure these keywords are listed throughout your resume or the applicant-tracking software the organization is using won't pull your resume in the search results.

4. Don't forget about branding

Branding your resume is important to your job search, but it is also vital to proving you're the perfect fit for an opening. You need to think about what makes you unique as a candidate. What can you offer that others can't? Show the employer you can offer them value and benefit that others cannot. Do this through a branding statement, branded career summary, and metrics-driven accomplishment statements.

Creating a resume that communicates your perfect fit for an open position can be challenging, but following these simple tips can make the process easier and less painstaking.

Source: Previously posted By: Jessica Holbrook Hernandez www.greatresumesfast.com

Subsection 4.1.e Five Ways to give your resume the WOW factor

In this tight job market, making your resume stand out is crucial. We all know that our resumes are our chief marketing tool, but still, there are many people who send out resumes that don't have what it takes to impress employers in the digital age. Years ago, a well-written, neatly typed resume could be photocopied and mailed out to companies with great success. The document was the same for each potential employer and it served as a written work history. Those days are gone.

In today's digital job market, a resume has to be internet-friendly. We have to understand and accept the fact that the document we email to employers will be subject to Google web searches and even scanned by an applicant tracking system. Although the change has made work easier for human resource departments, it makes things more difficult for a job seeker.

If you are struggling to find a job, here are 5 ways that you can add some "wow" to your digital resume:

1. **Research companies and keywords:** When starting your job search, look at job boards and print out all of the job listings for companies you are interested in. Compare the ads and look for the most frequently used keywords. These words will be related to the most desirable skills and experience for the position. Once

you've identified the important keywords, make sure that your resume contains those same words. Since most companies use some sort of applicant tracking system that scans resumes for specific keywords, the more hits your resume has, the better.

2. **Always customize your resume for the job:** The days of cookie-cutter resumes are long over, which is why it's important to edit your resume to match the keywords for each job. Every time you send out a resume, you should customize it to target the specific company. It's a little more effort, but if the prize is a job that will pay you a good salary, it's worth the extra 30 minutes. After all, this is the first deliverable to your new company—make it count.

3. **Address your cover letter to someone:** If you aren't sure who is in charge of hiring or don't know the name of the person, do some research and find out. These days, almost everyone has an online presence. With a quick web search or by using a professional networking site like LinkedIn, you should be able to discover the name of the person in charge of hiring. If your internet sleuthing doesn't give you a name, you could try cold calling the company and asking. Addressing a cover letter to "Dear Hiring Manager" should be avoided at all costs.

4. **Use your network to get a personal referral:** Having someone you know recommend you for the position is the best way to make sure that your resume is actually read by a real person. Once you submit your resume, make a list of people you know. If you don't personally know someone who works for the company, ask the people on your list if they know anyone. If, after checking with everyone, you still don't have a contact on the inside, use networking sites to find someone. Start a conversation and ask for help. You'll be surprised at how many people, even the ones you only know through distant friends, would be more than happy to help.

5. **Follow up with the hiring manager:** After sending in your resume and cover letter, it's a good idea to call the hiring manager personally to confirm that they have received your application. This doesn't mean that you should call and say, "Did you get my resume?" Instead, use the call as an opportunity to give your pitch and stand out. For example, you could call and say, "Hi, this is Ms. Smith. I've been working in sales for 10 years and I have a proven track record of success. I'm very interested in working with your company. I just sent you a copy of my resume. I wanted to take a moment to touch base with you and make sure that you've received it." This gives you a moment to state your name and say why you are someone they don't want to miss out on. It shows that you are determined and sincere about your interest in the position and illustrates how you get things done.

Giving your resume the "wow" factor involves doing more work at first, but it can make you stand out and help you land the job you really want.

Source: Previously Posted By: *Melissa Kennedy* http://www.beyond.com/MelissaKennedy-MD

Subsection 4.1.f Six key areas recruiters pay the most attention to on your resume

Ever wondered to yourself what the most critical areas are on your resume when a recruiter is giving it the initial review? As a former hiring manager, I will tell you exactly where I'm looking when I review your resume. However, don't just take my word for it; a recent study on recruiter behavior conducted by The Ladders confirms exactly what I'm about to tell you ... recruiters spend the most time reviewing the following areas:

1. **Your contact information.** Believe it or not, this is critical in a recruiter's search. Mostly because they want to ensure you're located near the position for which they're recruiting so that you can easily make it to interviews—and also not have a ridiculously long commute to work.

2. **Your most recent job title.** I believe this is why it's so important to put a job target/ job title at the top of your resume. It makes vital information easily accessible to recruiters so that they don't have to spend too much time searching for it.

   That being said, they will scan down your resume and look at the most logical place your previous employment would be listed. What they are looking for here is relevancy to your most recent positions. Have you previously been in this position?

3. **Dates of employment.** When I was a recruiter I was trained to not call anyone with fewer than nine months of job longevity at previous employers. Fewer than nine months indicates that you may be a job hopper—which makes you a potential risk to that recruiter.

4. **Primary Job Accomplishments/Responsibilities.** You can say a lot about what your previous duties were just by simply writing accomplishment-based statements on your resume. Attach numbers or metrics to everything when possible. Don't just tell them you improved sales; tell them by how much. Don't just say you can retain customers; show them you can by providing your retention rates.

5. **Keywords/Core Strengths.** Most recruiters will scan a bulleted keyword section at the top of your resume to find matching keywords from the position they are

trying to fill. Make sure your resume includes the most relevant keywords, and put this section at the top of your resume. Don't make the recruiter go searching for it.

6. **Education.** You can almost guarantee the recruiter is going to be looking at the bottom of your resume to find out if you have the credentials the position requires. If you don't hold the minimal level of education or certifications for the position, you may be considered weeded out.

Source: Previously posted By: Jessica Holbrook Hernandez www.greatresumesfast.com

Subsection 4.1.g Why her resume was not generating calls for interviews?

To understand why your resume isn't getting any callbacks, you first have to ask yourself a few questions. First, are you applying for jobs that you're qualified for? If yes, are you customizing your resume each time you apply for jobs you're qualified for? If you're not, If you are tailoring your resume to the position using "Tips for Making Your Resume a Perfect Match" and you're completely qualified for the job, then let's explore some other reasons.

Job Board and Applying Online

Online and using job boards is a numbers game. Unfortunately, with unemployment hanging around 8% for what feels like forever now, the reality is that the numbers are against you. There are lots of other candidates who may be just as qualified applying for the exact same role. Need a solution? Diversify your search. Don't just apply online on job boards. Use other means to job search. Need examples? LinkedIn, Twitter, Facebook—in other words, social net-working. Get out there and start making connections.

Going Offline

You can't stay inside on the computer all the time. Sometimes you have to get out and meet some people. Have you logged off the computer and set out to meet some people face to face? What about networking meetings, association meetings, or just chatting up a neighbor or the person in line at the grocery store? You never know when you'll meet someone who might have a connection that could get your foot in the door.

Are You Trying Anything Different?

Yes, networking online and off can be excellent ways to meet decision makers or get names, but have you tried anything different? For example, when I returned to work after staying home with my oldest for a year after she was born I knew I wanted to get right back into staffing. So what did I do? I looked up the addresses for every staffing agency and recruiting firm within a 25-mile radius of my house, and I mailed them a copy of my resume and cover letter. Sure, it may take a little extra time, but ultimately I received several callbacks, had some great interviews, and accepted a new position!

If you're using a well-written resume, applying for jobs you're qualified for, and customizing your resume to each application, chances are it's not your resume at all—it's your job search technique. Making a few small changes could mean the difference between no calls and your next great opportunity!

Source: Previously Posted By: Jessica Holbrook Hernandez www.greatresumesfast.com

➤ Section 5.1 Resume thoughts to keep this in mind

Subsection 5.1.a How changing your attitude can improve your resume

As job seekers, it's easy to believe that the process of looking for work is a cut-and-dried experience. You look for a job, type up your resume and cover letter, score an interview, and win the job. It's easy, right? Well, not quite.

Actually, a lot of time and effort go into the job-seeking process—and how you feel about that process is not exempt from affecting the outcome. Believe it or not, your attitude about the job search could have an adverse effect on how you write your resume. And, of course, if your resume isn't good, you most likely will not get the job. So how can you keep a good attitude about the job search?

Avoid Negative Thinking

While creating a resume may seem like a process that isolates itself from your feelings, nothing could be further from the truth. In fact, if you're feeling "blah" about the job search, you're likely to write a "blah" resume.

On the other hand, if you feel passionate about the job you're applying for, you're more likely to think "what can I write to make this company believe I *really* want this job?" and you naturally begin brainstorming ideas to help deliver your message.

Try your best to adopt a good attitude about your prospects for employment—and watch your resume blossom.

Feel Proud of Your Skills

Another attitude adjustment that could help your resume is feeling proud of your skills. If you really take a look at the skills you bring to the table and accomplishments you'd like to share, it can feel pretty exciting to think that an employer will look at your resume and say, "This is who we've been looking for!"

So how can you connect your skills and accomplishments to the job you're applying for? Comb through the company's job posting to see what the employer is looking for in a candidate, then proudly piece together your professional history in a way that shows you have the talent needed to surpass its goal.

Envision a Successful Career

It's also a great idea to develop a positive attitude that reaches beyond the job you're applying for and encompasses your entire career. It's good to think about how the role you want could provide opportunities for you to grow as a person and help you to develop into an expert in your field. Although this information doesn't need to be incorporated into your resume, it can work wonders in helping you to envision how you can make improvements to both the company and your career.

The words you write on your resume are a direct reflection of the way you feel about your prospects as a candidate for any position you apply for. If you don't believe you'll get the job, it will show. So find ways to feel good as you connect to each job you want. This can help you to write a convincing resume that scores you an interview.

Source: Previously posted By: Jessica Holbrook Hernandez www.greatresumesfast.com

Subsection 5.1.b Five mistakes that make your resume look bad

We all know how important our resumes are. In most cases, a resume is the first piece of our work that an employer will ever see. This means that every detail is saying something about who we are, how we present ourselves and why we would be a good choice for the position. Because of that, it's crucial that our resumes paint the best picture possible.

There are some mistakes that we all know not to do—like spelling and grammar errors, but there are others that you may not have even considered. To help you make your resume be the best it can be, here are 5 common mistakes that make your resume look bad:

1. **Not including contact information**—During your job search, you should have multiple versions of your resume. Depending on the type of jobs you're applying for, you may have several. However, everyone should have an online version and a more complete version. The difference is that the resume you use on social networking and job search sites shouldn't have actual contact information for your previous employers or references. Also, you shouldn't include your home address

and phone number. That being said, when you apply for a job, be sure that your resume includes your email address in the header. Remember that you need to provide some way for the employer to get in touch with you.

2. **Too long; Didn't Read**—An effective resume should be about one page long. If you have been in the workforce for a long time and have held many jobs, you may need to go up to two pages. Typically, a resume that is longer than two pages probably isn't going to be read. Many hiring managers are in a hurry to narrow down their list of applicants and don't have the time to read through a long resume.

3. **Overwhelming Design**—There has been a growing trend toward creative resumes that use design elements to make an impression. For example, if you are a graphic designer, having a clever resume that demonstrates your design aesthetic can be a great way to make an impression. However, for most resumes, using a template or design that is too overpowering or uses non-standard fonts can limit your chances at getting a job offer. Depending on the word processing program the employer uses, your resume might not be view-able or it might look like gibberish.

4. **Too difficult to read**—Using long paragraphs makes your resume harder to read. To avoid this, the judicious use of bullet points can make the information more readily apparent to the reader. Also, using bullet points will allow you to cut out the unnecessary details and information that the employer isn't interested in.

5. **Using the wrong format**—Every business has a different computer system and there is no way for you to know what word processing program they use. There are so many programs in use today, and not everyone uses Microsoft Word. To be safe, be sure that your digital resume is saved in a .txt, .pdf or .doc format. This way, you can be relatively certain that your file will be able to be opened by almost anyone. Making sure that your resume sparkles is the best way to increase your chances of getting the job you want.

Source: Previously Posted By: *Melissa Kennedy* http://www.beyond.com/MelissaKennedy-MD

Subsection 5.1.c Nine words to dump from your resume and the 9 Hot to include

Think of the hundreds of resumes that cross an HR manager's desk every week. It's truly a mountain of paperwork they'd rather bypass. With the job market being what it is, applicants and recent grads are cranking out resumes using the same accepted industry standard formats. Nothing wrong with that. But there are subtle ways to make your resume stand out from the rest.

One way is to be word wise. That means dumping the standard weak-weasel words and "amping" your resume with power words. Words that will catch a recruiter's or HR manager's eye. Words that will stop a keyword scanning program and shift your resume into the "take a second look" category. But first, the words that need dumping.

They include:

1. Strong
2. Exceptional
3. Good
4. Excellent
5. Outstanding
6. Effective
7. Driven
8. Motivated
9. Seasoned

These are self-aggrandizing words that your references may use to describe you. But if you use them, it sounds like you're patting yourself on the back. They simply lack objectivity. They're qualitative and can't easily be linked to quantitative appraisals of your accomplishments.

It's much better to use the hot 9 words that can be connected to specific areas of your performance on the job. These will catch a recruiter's or HR manager's eye. They'll also be flagged by keyword programs, giving your resume a "second read." They include:

1. Reduced
2. Improved
3. Developed
4. Researched
5. Created
6. Increased
7. Accomplished
8. Won
9. Under budget

When using these keywords, try to link them with specific facts and figures. This adds credibility to the words and will draw the attention of recruiters, HR managers and most recently, applicant tracking software.

It's an unfortunate fact of life that most companies now use some type of applicant tracking software. This software looks for keywords that match specific job requirements. Some companies digitize the hundreds of resumes they receive on a daily basis, store them in a database, search for candidates using keywords, and then create interview call lists. The bottom line: If your resume lacks the right combination of job-specific keywords, it will end up in digital limbo, never to be seen again until a programmer purges the file. I know, it's brutal and impersonal, but such is the world we live in.

Here are some suggestions on the types of keywords to include in your resume. They should be job, task and industry specific:

1. Job Titles
2. Product Names
3. Technical Terms
4. Industry Jargon
5. Software/Hardware Packages
6. Job-specific Buzzwords
7. Degrees or Certifications
8. University or College Names
9. Company Names
10. Service Types
11. Professional Organizations

Creating an effective resume that will get noticed these day's takes a bit of work. Much more than just listing your accomplishments.

Source: Previously Posted By: *Alex Kecskes* www.akcreativeworks.com

Subsection 5.1.d Why your resume isn't helping you get hired

A resume is a critical element in your job search. In fact, it is the key to *helping* you to get hired for a position. It's important to emphasize "help" because the resume typically doesn't get you hired—but it does *help* you to score an interview where you can then impress employers enough so that they want to offer you the job.

So, if you're not getting called in for interviews, what is it about your resume that isn't doing the trick? Let's take a look at some of the reasons why your resume may not be helping you to get hired.

It Never Makes It past the Scanning Technology

As a persistent job seeker, you may be aware that many companies utilize scanning technology that helps them to eliminate resumes that don't fit the criteria of the position. With so many applicants submitting resumes, it can be challenging and time consuming to sift through dozens that won't make the cut.

The scanning technology helps to eliminate this problem by filtering out resumes that don't list specific words or phrases that align with the position. For instance, in the nursing field, you might work in a health care facility, participate in transplant procedures, or work with people with mental illnesses. If this is true, these phrases should be listed in your resume to identify you as a qualified candidate.

As you write your resume, be sure to review the job posting thoroughly for these keywords, and list them strategically throughout your resume. This way, you won't be bypassed in the very first step of the hiring process.

Your Resume Isn't Targeted

If you've written a resume that incorporates the correct keywords, it may just make it past the scanning technology. In that case, great job! But your work is not finished. Another reason why your resume may not be getting you any interview calls is that it isn't targeted.

A targeted resume is one that was written specifically for the company you're applying with. If you search online, you'll find a multitude of resume samples and templates to help you get the process started. But they aren't authentic—it's up to you to create your own resume that speaks directly to a company.

So if you want to use a template for inspiration, there's nothing wrong with it; however, you need to create your own original resume in the end. Doing so proves that your skills and accomplishments directly align with the qualifications each company is looking for.

Your Experience Isn't Convincing Enough

Another issue that could prevent the interview callback is a lack of convincing experience. You may be accustomed to listing skills but haven't shown that you were a leader who initiated projects or worked above and beyond the call of duty in your previous positions. So take time to list specific accomplishments that show you made a difference.

Once you target your resume, add keywords, and list top-notch experience, you're on the right track. Taking these steps is a tremendous aid in getting you the interview callback.

Source: Previously posted By: Jessica Holbrook Hernandez www.greatresumesfast.com

Subsection 5.1.e Exaggerated resumes can quickly ruin your job search

As you can imagine, lying on your resume is always a no-no. If you feel you must avoid the truth, then you are probably applying for the wrong job. But what if you want to just exaggerate a bit—such as switching your title to one that sounds more impressive? Or stating that you won an award that you were only nominated for?

The truth is, no matter how you slice it, there's nothing to gain from exaggerating on your resume. But if exaggerating is out of the question, how can you make yourself sound more impressive? Take a look at a few ways you can make improvements to your overall job search without stretching the truth.

Use Action-Oriented Descriptions

Rather than relying on a skill you do not possess—or an accomplishment belonging to someone else—to improve your resume, try finding better ways to describe your current qualifications. This involves moving away from a responsibilities/duties-driven resume to one that is action-oriented.

For instance, suppose one of your primary roles was to file documents but you also had a great idea to develop a new filing system for your department—a goal you completed on your own. On your resume, rather than writing: "Was responsible for filing documents," write "Initiated and developed a new filing system utilized by the entire legal department."

In this case, the description is still true but offers more insight into your leadership capabilities.

Beef Up Your Cover Letter

Assuming you have included a cover letter with your application for employment, you can utilize this tool as a way to back up claims made in your resume while creating a more vivid picture of who you are as a job candidate.

Beefing up your cover letter can include telling a story about your love of the field and how you reached your current level of success. Or you could tell a specific story about a challenge you overcame and what you learned from it; this could provide the hiring manager with a sense of your diligence and also display your commitment to the position and your field as a whole.

Work to Improve Your Qualifications

If you're not happy with your current qualifications, take time to improve them. Enroll in training courses or college classes that can show your willingness to improve your skills—and, of course, list your progress on your resume. This way, employers will recognize your dedication and your willingness to boost your value as a candidate.

Remember, exaggerating your qualifications on your resume is always dangerous. Employers have amazing ways of checking out your background, so the last thing you want to do is represent yourself as someone you're not.

Instead, take pride in your current qualifications while working to improve those you lack. The fact that you're working toward becoming a more qualified professional could be quite impressive to a hiring manager looking for an honest and well-qualified employee.

Source: Previously posted By: Jessica Holbrook Hernandez www.greatresumesfast.com

Subsection 5.1.f Taking a conversational approach to writing your resume

Oftentimes, writing a resume can be difficult because we have a hard time connecting on a personal level to what we're writing. While we may relate to the skills we possess, we often take a bit of a mechanical approach when delivering the message.

A great way to begin the process of drafting your resume without getting caught in robotic writing is to try taking a conversational approach. By envisioning that you're speaking to a person about your qualifications, you could add depth to your resume.

Write as If You Are Speaking to a Person

Many people don't internalize when they're writing their resumes the way they do when they're writing to an actual person. But writing a resume essentially is telling someone through words, "I'm the right person for this job."

How would you communicate that to a person if you were speaking to them face to face? Would you offer dry statements like, "I am responsible for managing sales representatives" or would you want to sell yourself by sharing how many sales representatives you manage, how much money you've earned for the company, and why you *love* your job?

You would likely opt for the latter. To mimic this in your resume, review a conversation like this in your mind, and then jot down ideas you might share as you write your draft.

Envision Questions a Manager Might Ask

Another great way to create your resume using a conversational approach is to envision the hiring manager or key decision maker in a company asking you questions about why you want the job.

Just imagine that you own a company. If you wanted people to work within your business, you would likely prefer they have a great deal of knowledge in the areas you're hiring for. In fact, you'd love it if they brought exceptional expertise to the table so that you can move the company ahead of the curve.

As you can imagine, a hiring manager is looking for the same from you. So think of questions a manager might ask you, then come up with colorful responses—keeping your own "company" in mind.

This could help you align yourself with the true goals of the position and inspire you to share information you believe could propel the company in new and exciting directions.

Read Your Resume With a Friend

Finally, take time to read your resume to a few people and watch their reactions to your qualifications. Do they react as though they're impressed by your accomplishments, or are they bored? Get their feedback to help improve your resume.

After you've drafted your resume from a conversational perspective, then you can go back and give it a professional tone—but have colorful adjectives and action verbs in your arsenal.

This approach can help you remember that your resume is designed to deliver a message that you're the right person for the job. There's no better way to get this done than through the colorful language of a conversation.

Source: Previously Posted By: Jessica Holbrook Hernandez www.greatresumesfast.com

➤ Section 6.1 Executive Resume Tips

Subsection 6.1. a Are writing mechanics making or breaking your executive resume?

There are so many essentials to consider when writing an executive resume that sometimes it can be easy to overlook critical elements of the writing process. One often overlooked element is writing mechanics.

Paying attention to writing mechanics can include making sure your sentences are correctly structured, words are not misspelled, word choice is correct, and the document does not contain any obvious grammatical errors. As you can imagine, making too many mistakes on your resume could result in its being tossed. So what are some ways you can avoid making mistakes when developing and finalizing your resume?

Check the Spelling and Grammar

Although spelling and grammar is usually the last items on your things-to-do list when developing your resume, they need to be moved into a priority position before you submit the document. Why? Hiring decision makers have to read resumes all day, and when reading, the last thing they want to do is run across a sentence like this:

"Highly successful in building client relationship that drive margin increases a cost reduction."

While the errors can be viewed as minor, they could easily annoy a person who has to read resumes all day and is interested in seeing only perfection.

Of course, the best way to avoid minor slip-ups is to proofread your resume until you feel certain that it is error-free. Also, you can hand it over to a few friends to have them help you proofread it some more.

Examine Readability and Repetition

In developing your resume; you also want to avoid repeating the same words and phrases over and over again. While you may not be expected to come to the table with an amazing vocabulary, you at least want to showcase some variety in your descriptive phrases and action words so that employers can discern just how dynamic a candidate you are.

Also, it's important to be sure that your resume reads well in terms of sentence structure as well as the overall format. If your sentences are too long and confusing, or if the resume is too dense and lacking in white space, it could be difficult to convince an employer that your document is worth reading.

Sometimes it's hard to believe that the fundamentals of writing are just as important as the qualifications you include in your resume. But if you are able to manage the mechanics of writing *and* share your amazing qualifications, you will have a better chance of impressing your prospective employers as they read your resume.

Source: Previously Posted By: Jessica Holbrook Hernandez www.greatresumesfast.com

Subsection 6.1.b Are you over qualified? Why not edit your resume?

There are times, like when you are trying to make a career change, when applying for a job you're overqualified for makes sense. The problem is that it can be a challenge to be taken seriously for an entry-level job when you have a master's degree. As strange as it seems, in those cases, your past successes can be the very thing that's holding you back.

In general, it's not a good idea to apply for jobs that you're overqualified for. For one, it's not likely that you'll be happy with the job long term and many employers will be hesitant to take a chance on you. However, if you're changing careers, you have to start at the bottom. So what can you do to minimize the problem and get the entry level job you want?

It's simple—Edit your resume.

Your resume doesn't have to be a linear history of your job history. Instead, it can be a functional resume, which only lists your relevant work experience. If you choose this type of format, you can feel free to leave out the things that will hurt your chances at getting the job. Here are a few other things you can do:

Remove job titles—If your previous positions were significantly senior to the entry level position you're applying for, remove the job title from your resume. This way, instead of your resume stating that you were the VP of Sales, it will just say Sales.

Remove your highest degree—There are some experts who suggest that you should remove the highest level degree you have from your resume. By doing so, you'll lower your chances of being ruled out before you have had a chance to interview.

Don't lie—Never outright lie on your resume. Information is too easy to check and it will make you look bad. However, dumbing your resume down and leaving out information like your previous salary history might be a good option.

Source: Previously Posted By: *Melissa Kennedy* http://www.beyond.com/MelissaKennedy-MD

Subsection 6.1.c Executive resume too short—Here are some ways to lengthen it

There are many challenges to being an executive job seeker. It's likely that one of the biggest is that you have been employed for so long that you don't remember how to search for work anymore. Not to mention that the job-seeking world may have changed significantly since your last seeking experience.

But another challenge some executives struggle with could be unique to others: the short resume. If you are a candidate who has experience with only one or two companies, you may feel uncomfortable submitting a resume that looks like it could belong to an entry-level professional.

It's true that executive resumes are typically a bit lengthy due to the excess of qualifications acquired over the years. So if you're working with a one-pager, here are some ideas to help stretch it out.

Spread Out Your History

If you are working with the history of only one or two employers, it's possible that your entire resume may stretch out to only one or one and a half pages. In order to give your resume some length (and depth), it's good to dig into your history to find ways to spread it out some.

For instance, rather than listing only your executive positions in your resume, provide an overview of your rise to the position by listing your roles within the companies you worked for.

List each position, the title, and years worked—then note any top-notch accomplishments that helped you to get promoted. Be sure to briefly explain what it was that helped bump you up to the next level. This will not only stretch out your resume but also give employers greater insight into why your career has been so successful.

Choose (Slightly) Larger Font Sizes

If you are utilizing two or three different font sizes throughout your resume, consider upping the size of each one—little by little—to see how much length you get. Start with just a one-half font-size increase (i.e., 11 to 11.5) to see how much the resume stretches. Then step it up another half-point to see the difference that makes. Of course, you don't want to make the resume fonts too large because then the hiring decision makers are likely to notice—so be careful not to increase the sizes too much.

Increase Line Spacing

Another way to give your resume more length is to increase the line spacing. Whether you're jumping from single spacing to 1.5, or only adjusting the spacing between paragraphs, these subtle changes can make a difference in the length of your resume, and can even create more white space—which is a good thing.

But like font sizes, avoid increasing the spacing too much. It's much better to add more content to your resume than to rely on formatting tricks.

Unfortunately, the job-seeking world is one that judges books by their covers more often than not. So while your history as an executive might be very impressive, the appearance that you have no history at all could stop your search in its tracks.

It's true that executive resumes are typically a bit lengthy due to the excess of qualifications acquired over the years. So if you're working with a one-pager, here are some ideas to help stretch it out.

Spread Out Your History

If you are working with the history of only one or two employers, it's possible that your entire resume may stretch out to only one or one and a half pages. In order to give your resume some length (and depth), it's good to dig into your history to find ways to spread it out some. For instance, rather than listing only your executive positions in your resume, provide an overview of your rise to the position by listing your roles within the companies you worked for.

List each position, the title, and years worked—then note any top-notch accomplishments that helped you to get promoted. Be sure to briefly explain what it was that helped bump you up to the next level. This will not only stretch out your resume but also give employers greater insight into why your career has been so successful.

Choose (Slightly) Larger Font Sizes

If you are utilizing two or three different font sizes throughout your resume, consider upping the size of each one—little by little—to see how much length you get. Start with just a one-half font-size increase (i.e., 11 to 11.5) to see how much the resume stretches. Then step it up another half-point to see the difference that makes.

Of course, you don't want to make the resume fonts too large because then the hiring decision makers are likely to notice—so be careful not to increase the sizes too much. Another way to give your resume more length is to increase the line spacing. Whether you're jumping from single spacing to 1.5, or only adjusting the spacing between paragraphs, these subtle changes can make a difference in the length of your resume, and can even create more white space—which is a good thing.

But like font sizes, avoid increasing the spacing too much. It's much better to add more content to your resume than to rely on formatting tricks.

Unfortunately, the job-seeking world is one that judges books by their covers more often than not. So while your history as an executive might be very impressive, the appearance that you have no history at all could stop your search in its tracks.

Source: Previously posted By: Jessica Holbrook Hernandez www.greatresumesfast.com

➢ Section 7.1 Miscellaneous

Subsection 7.1.a Why employers use an applicant tracking system

If you've taken the time to customize your resume, write a great cover letter and submit your applications, everything is out of your hands. But, what happens to your resume after you hit send? You might be surprised to learn that almost all employers, even very small companies, use an applicant tracking system.

So, why is this important?

If you understand the process, you're much more likely to be asked for an interview. Many people still believe that most companies have hiring managers who read through every resume and make a decision about who they want to contact. This couldn't be further from the truth. Today, it's so easy to use a screening program.

These programs sort through all of the resumes looking for keywords that apply to the position. The screening program will eliminate resumes from people who don't match the criteria, leaving only the most suitable matches for the hiring manager to look over. It saves the company time and money, making the hiring process more streamlined.

Although the applicant tracking system may rule out resumes from people who are actually qualified, it leaves the ones that understand how the process works.

So, why do employers use these systems if they miss some qualified applicants?

There are too many resumes to read

Especially now with the tight job market, employers are being flooded with applications for just a handful of job openings. It's estimated that most employers receive about 1,000 applicants for each job posting. Added to that, job boards have made applying for jobs very easy and quick, which means that unqualified people aren't risking much by applying for jobs they don't expect to get. The applicant tracking system can quickly go through the stack and narrow the list down to just the people who are truly interested in the job and who have the necessary skills.

Prevents discrimination and charges of misconduct

There are many laws on the books that prevent employers from discriminating against job seekers because of their age, gender, ethnicity and more. For most companies, it's important to show that they aren't using any of that information to disqualify otherwise acceptable applicant. This is where the applicant tracking system really comes in handy. Because a non-biased computer program is sorting through the resumes, there's no chance that a hiring manager could be swayed, even without realizing it, by any of these factors. The system also allows companies to quickly show that they are complying with all federal laws.

They save money

There are lots of different applicant tracking programs. Some of them are free, while others are not as expensive as hiring someone to read over all of the resumes. Because they are easy for even a small business to use, they are a good investment. The low cost, combined with high results means that this type of screening is probably here to stay.

The good news is that once you understand how the applicant tracking system works and why almost every company uses them, it's easier to make your resume stand out. Be sure to use the same keywords in your resume and cover letter that the company used in the job listing. If they list specific requirements, make sure that you have them listed clearly so that your resume won't end up in the trash pile.

Source: Previously Posted By: *Melissa Kennedy* http://www.beyond.com/MelissaKennedy-MD

Subsection 7.1.b Should you hire a resume writer?

When you're looking for a job, it's hard to know if you should take a chance and hire a resume writer, or if you can get away with doing it yourself. It's a tough call. On one hand, I've seen many really great resumes that were self-written. On the other hand, your resume is too important to leave up to chance. So, what can you do?

If you prefer to write your resume on your own, don't just trust yourself to give it the polished look that you want. Go to your local library or bookstore and read books about resume writing. Often, they have samples you can look at and they can be an invaluable resource. Just focusing your energy on making your resume better is enough to get the wheels of creativity turning.

One thing you'll notice fairly quickly is that the suggestions will vary wildly from book to book and sometimes the advice from one book to another can be contradicting.

It's important to know a little about what you want your end result to look like so that you'll be able to pick and choose the tips that work best for you. You should take into consideration your personality, your industry, your previous experience and the job for which you're applying.

Even if you write it yourself, it's a good idea to get a friend or someone you trust to read over your resume to look for grammar and spelling errors. Little mistakes are so easy to make and can be really tricky to find. However, if you ask for advice, be prepared to hear and accept constructive criticism.

That isn't to say that you have to make every change that they suggest, but it does mean that you have to listen to their thoughts with an open mind. Thank them for their help and whatever you do, don't make them feel attacked or upset about anything they said about your resume. You don't have to take their advice, but you do have to hear it and be respectful. Don't forget that you asked for their help because they were someone you trusted. Maybe their opinion is worth giving some extra thought to.

If you have trouble with spelling and grammar, don't take chances. If you can afford it, hire someone to help you write your resume. You can usually find a resume writer online, in the classified and even in the phone book.

You can even do a Google search and find people more than willing to help you make your resume really stand out. Before you choose a writer, you'll want to talk about work styles, what their time frame is, how much they charge and if they provide other services like cover letters and thank you notes.

Be sure to get a sample of the writer's work to review before you make a decision. You'll want to select someone whom you are comfortable working with and who you think could have a voice sort of like yours. Since you want your resume to capture your personality, make sure that your writer is up to the task.

Whichever way you decide to go, your resume should be a reflection of who you are. Most of the time, it's the very first thing that an employer sees from you and it is the reason that you'll get invited to an interview. Make it count.

Source: Previously Posted By: *Melissa Kennedy* http://www.beyond.com/MelissaKennedy-MD

Subsection 7.1.c The truth about job references

When applying for a job, it's not just your resume and interview that matter. Who you select to be your reference can make a huge difference. For me, picking the right reference has always been a challenge. There was a time, years ago, when I was applying for a job with a company that also employed a friend of the family.

Before I submitted my application, I asked the friend if they would be willing to put in a good word for me.

Because of our family connection, I didn't think that my request was inappropriate. She said that she would be happy to help. Thinking that everything would be fine, I went ahead and applied for the job. During the interview, I gave her name as a reference. I was offered the job on the spot and went home feeling victorious. Unfortunately, my victory was short-lived.

A few hours later, I received a phone call from the hiring manager saying that he checked with my reference and because of that, he was forced to take back the job offer.

At first, I thought he had to be kidding, but soon I realized that my friend wasn't as happy to help as she had claimed and in fact, didn't like me at all. It was an eye-opening experience to say the least, and one that can be prevented by making sure that your references are rock solid.

So, how can you make sure that the references you provide a new employer are going to be effective? Well, here are a few **truths** about job references that can make the task a little easier:

While your previous employers have some restrictions about what they are able to say, they can and will give you a bad reference if warranted—Many Human Resource offices have policies in place that prevent them from giving bad references, however, these rules can be bent.

Not only that, there are still ways to get the point across without violating any rules. For example, simply saying "Please check this person's references very carefully" or "Let me pull the legal file to be sure what I'm allowed to say" is enough to make a prospective employer think twice.

Only provide references when specifically asked—You should treat your references like gold. Don't give away their contact information without good reason. Most of us send out copies of our resumes to companies we never hear from again, so there is no need to hand over this sensitive information.

Instead, wait until the interview to provide them, that way, you'll have more control over who contacts them and why.

Stay in touch with your references—If you've had a professor, a mentor or a boss who worked closely with you, keep in touch with them. This doesn't mean that you have to talk to them every day, but you should stay in contact and update them with information about your career and accomplishments. After all, you want them to have all of the relevant info about what you're doing now, rather than only being able to speak about the past. In addition, staying in contact helps build the friendship, making it more likely that they will have positive things to say about you.

Always ask before using someone as a reference—This one is huge. Don't assume that someone will give you a good reference. In fact, it's not enough to simply ask them in casual conversation, you have to take things a step farther and ask what sort of reference they would give you. In my case, even though I asked, I made the mistake of asking while we were in the company of other family members.

Without realizing it, I put her on the spot and she agreed only because saying no would have been rude. Instead, I should have pulled her aside and mentioned why I was looking for the job and talked about my qualifications. Then, I should have asked her if there was anything she could do to help me get the job and if I could use her for a reference.

When in doubt, you should do a test run—This may sound silly, but if you aren't sure what your references will say about you, why not does a test run? This is exactly what it sounds like. Enlist a friend's help, pretend to be a prospective employer and ask for a reference. It might seem sneaky, but it will give you a better idea of what an employer will learn about you.

Keep in mind that just because you get the job, it doesn't mean that you're done. Employers can, and often do, use the 90-day probation period to conduct more intensive background checks. During that time, if your work abilities or your references don't make you stand out, your new boss can fire you without having to give an explanation.

Source: Previously Posted By: *Melissa Kennedy* http://www.beyond.com/MelissaKennedy-MD

Subsection 7.1.d Irreplaceable employees—7 Questions

Is there a way to become the type of employee that your employer just can't afford to let go? Is it possible for you to know *so much* that your employer would *do anything* to avoid losing you? Here are seven questions you can ask yourself—and also use to evaluate yourself as an employee—to determine if you're irreplaceable at work.

1. Are you adaptable?

Flexible employees can adjust and make changes as the company makes changes. They're not stale or stuck in their ways and employers know they can count on these employees to make the adjustments necessary to keep the company running.

2. Are you progressive?

Do you come up with new ideas, new ways to save time or money, or promote the company so that it's profitable and steadfast?

3. Are you willing to do whatever is necessary?

Employers want to know they can count on you to not only do your part and your job, but also pitch in when necessary, pick up the slack, or stay late if needed.

4. Are you learning new skills?

Employees who learn new skills on the job are pretty valuable to the organization. If you're constantly improving yourself and your performance, then you're becoming an invaluable asset to the company.

5. Are you processing new information and applying it?

Are you applying the new skills you've learned or any new information you've gleaned about the business? What are you doing with the information that has been given to you by your employer? Some employees just take the information in and never do anything with it. Others are doers: they take what they've learned and apply it to make situations, circumstances, and organizations run better.

6. Are you controlling the information you take in?

Information can be distracting or empowering. Are you the type of employee who sends 100 e-mails a day but never gets any real work done or never takes action to resolve the problem? Don't be controlled. Use what you know to empower yourself to make changes and make things better.

7. Do you solve problems?

Employees who *solve* problems are almost never let go—while employees who *create* problems are almost always terminated.

Consider these seven questions—and take a good, hard look at your work ethic and how you operate within your organization. While not all-inclusive or the end-all, be-all of who gets cut and who stays, these seven steps can help you to make yourself an invaluable and irreplaceable employee.

Source: Previously posted By: Jessica Holbrook Hernandez www.greatresumesfast.com

➤ **Section 8.1** Cover and Outreach Letters: Example of Introduction Letters

---

Dear Mr. Applicant

I recommend you keep the letters document intact—copying and pasting to make specific changes from one to another, or set up each letter as a master document in a merge file. When you do copy a letter to become a new document, be sure to remove all the notes, titles and instructions before you make a final draft.

Please use your own words which will make these letters sound like you. Your selection, sentence structure, etc. should all be natural sounding, not as though they were taken from a book.

Source: S. Brennan

Subsection 8.1.a Letter #1 Informational Interview Request—No Resume

Ima Kneedy
1234 Any Street Drive NW
My City, WA 98335
222-XXX-XXXX
somebody@internet.com

Decision Maker, Title
Company Name
Address
City, State Zip

Dear Name of Decision Maker:

I am currently in the process of exploring new career options. In order to determine my next move, I would like to establish contact with a variety of professionals within the XXXX industry. In your position you undoubtedly learn of activities in your industry long before there is any press about them. Thus, I would very much appreciate the opportunity to tap into your professional network. Perhaps you know of one or two other people who would also be interested in an exchange of information.

By way of introduction,

The opportunity to network and exchange ideas would be all I ask. To minimize any inconvenience to you, I will call your office next week to introduce myself and schedule a brief (10-15 minute) meeting. I really appreciate any ideas you have to offer.

Sincerely,

Subsection 8.1.b Letter #2 Advice—No Resume

Ima Kneedy
1234 Any Street Drive NW
My City, WA 98335
222-XXX-XXXX
somebody@internet.com

Date

Decision Maker, Title
Company Name
Address
City, State Zip

Dear Name of Decision Maker:

I recently began exploring career options and I realized someone with your background might provide me with some assistance. I am writing to ask you for some input on the possibilities of utilizing my skills within the XXXX field.

I would like to ask you to take a few minutes from your hectic schedule to meet with me so that I can glean some advice, information and suggestions as to where and how I might contribute. To relieve any pressure you may be feeling, please understand that I am not soliciting a job. You are a leader in your field and I know your ideas would be of great value to me.

By way of introduction, my career has provided opportunities for me to be an integral participant in XXXXXX.

If convenient, I would like to meet briefly with you in the next week. I will call your office in a few days to see if we can schedule a short meeting.

Thank you very much for your time and attention. I look forward to speaking with you personally.

Sincerely,

Subsection 8.1.c Letter #3 Direct Employer—Targeted—No Resume Included

Ima Kneedy
1234 Any Street Drive NW
My City, WA 98335
222-XXX-XXXX
somebody@internet.com

Date

Decision Maker, Title
Company Name
Address
City, State Zip

Dear Name of Decision Maker:

Currently a XXXXXXXX in a XXXXXX, I am exploring other opportunities in which to invest my time and experience. In reviewing other companies with the intent of forming a new affiliation, yours aroused my curiosity and interest. I am seeking an organization preparing to grow to the next level of success, a company that embraces the planning and preparation needed to capitalize on opportunity.

By way of introduction, my career has provided opportunities for me to be an integral participant in XXXXX.

My corner stone in developing or implementing any project has always involved the same process: seeking an overview of the whole and a close-up of the parts, evaluating available data, devising strategy, leading and motivating the participants and performing the tasks critical to success. My track record aptly represents the effectiveness of the approach.

Perhaps we should meet and discuss your company's future and how I can contribute to your plans. I will call your office in a few days so we can arrange a convenient time. I look forward to meeting with you and sharing a few moments of your time.

Sincerely,

Subsection 8.1.d Letter # 4 Events-Can be used as a direct approach Letter—Resume or for Spot Opportunities

Ima Kneedy
1234 Any Street Drive NW
My City, WA 98335
222-XXX-XXXX
somebody@internet.com

Date

Decision Maker, Title
Company Name
Address
City, State Zip

Dear Name of Decision Maker:

Last week's XXXXXX (or whatever your source) contained an interesting article about (name of company) which dealt with the likelihood of your expanding your investment portfolio (or whatever) to include (whatever). I was very excited about this new development to the point where I found myself wanting to be part of the plan. (DISCUSS THOSE SEGMENTS OF THE ARTICLE YOU FEEL PARTICULARLY WELL-QUALIFIED TO ADDRESS) That is why I am writing directly to you.

By way of introduction, my career has provided opportunities for me to be an integral participant in XXXXXX.

My cornerstone XXXXX.

A discussion of your plans and my background would provide insight into a possible association. I will call your office early next week to see if we can meet in order to explore things further. I look forward to talking with you.

Sincerely,

Subsection 8.1.e Letter # 5 ads, blind or identified—with or without resume

Ima Kneedy
1234 Any Street Drive NW
My City, WA 98335
222-XXX-XXXX
somebody@internet.com
Date

Decision Maker, Title
Company Name
Address
City, State Zip

Dear Name of Decision Maker:

Your recent advertisement for a XXXXXX indicates you have an exciting opportunity for the right individual. A discussion of my background and your needs should prove valuable to both of us.

By way of introduction, my career has provided opportunities for me to be an integral participant in XXXXXX

(ADD ADDITIONAL PROFESSIONAL CHARACTERISTICS, SKILLS, ETC IF SPECIFIED IN THE AD)

These look like the kind of attributes you require from the ideal candidate for the position. I would welcome the opportunity to meet with you, learn more about the specifics of this challenge and discuss the ways in which I believe I can meet them. Perhaps you can give me a call and we can arrange for a convenient time to meet.

Sincerely,

Enclosure

Here is how you might respond to a salary request: I will submit my salary history once you indicate a serious interest in my qualifications. Or you can respond with a range, i.e my compensation scale is between $55,000 & $85,000 and I'm currently above the mid-range point.

Subsection 8.1.f Letter #6 Alumni, Colleagues, Friends and Acquaintances—Resume Enclosed

Ima Kneedy
1234 Any Street Drive NW
My City, WA 98335
222-XXX-XXXX
somebody@internet.com

Date

Decision Maker, Title
Company Name
Address
City, State Zip

Dear Name of Decision Maker:

I have recently made the decision to make a career change and I am in the process of exploring new business options. I am hoping that you might offer me some advice and information.

Currently I am XXXXX. I am seeking a position (state future direction).

I would greatly appreciate your taking a moment to review the enclosed resume. Any names of individuals you feel I should contact would be extremely helpful, even those who may be able to direct me to others. The more people I can contact regarding this endeavor, the better my chances of uncovering what I am seeking. I am open to any avenues you suggest.

If you have any thoughts or ideas please jot them down. I will contact you in a week or so to discuss your ideas. Thank you in advance for your help.

Sincerely,

Enclosure

Subsection 8.1.g Letter #7 Search firms & employment agencies—Resume enclosed

Ima Kneedy
1234 Any Street Drive NW
My City, WA 98335
222-XXX-XXXX
somebody@internet.com

Date

Decision Maker, Title
Company Name
Address
City, State Zip

Dear Name of Decision Maker:

Your firm has come to my attention as one that frequently conducts client searches for qualified individuals with solid credentials in XXXXXXX.

To give you an indication of my qualifications, I am enclosing a copy of my resume, which details some of the more significant contributions I have made in my career.

If it appears that my qualifications meet the need of one of your clients, I will be happy to further discuss my background in a meeting with you or in an interview with your client. I look forward to hearing from you.

Sincerely,

Subsection 8.1.h Letter #8 Letter to References—Enclose Resume— Enclose List of References

Ima Kneedy
1234 Any Street Drive NW
My City, WA 98335
222-XXX-XXXX
somebody@internet.com

Date

Decision Maker, Title
Company Name
Address
City, State Zip

Dear Name of Decision Maker:

Thank you for your willingness to serve as a reference during my career search. I am very appreciative of your assistance.

As my campaign gains momentum, you will undoubtedly receive calls from potential employers with whom I have been in contact. I felt it would be helpful for you to have some information available that highlights my work experience and qualifications. Although you may be familiar with most of my background, I have attached a current resume for you to review. Hopefully, it will assist you in answering any questions.

I am also enclosing a list of others who have agreed to be references for me. Many potential employers will ask for additional names of individuals whom they may contact. I have sent each one of my references the same information I am enclosing for you. You may wish to consider one or more of these names when you are requested to provide additional references.

Thank you again for your support during my search campaign. I would appreciate your contacting me when there is activity from a potential employer.

In any event, I will be contacting you periodically to keep you advised of my progress.

Sincerely,

Enclosures—(Please list your references on a separate sheet of paper as attachment. Be sure you include names, addresses, telephone numbers, and email.

Subsection 8.1.i Letter #9 Follow-Up Interview—This should be mailed in 24 hours of your interview

Ima Kneedy
1234 Any Street Drive NW
My City, WA 98335
222-XXX-XXXX
somebody@internet.com

Date

Decision Maker, Title
Company Name
Address
City, State Zip

Dear Name of Decision Maker:

The position we discussed *Friday* offers considerable opportunity and challenge. After rethinking our discussion, I am convinced that I can make an immediate contribution toward the growth and profitability of *Company Name.*

The following accomplishments are related to our discussion and lend support to my ability to confidently meet any challenges related to this position:

1.
2.
3.

(Select examples that support the key areas of need that emerged during the interview)

I am convinced that my proven track record of increasing revenues in each of my past environments coupled with my skill at creating positive change can provide both the immediate and long term results you desire.

I am sincerely interested in an association with *Company Name.* Our discussion was both insightful and productive. Your environment provides the challenges I am seeking and in which I have always been successful. I look forward to speaking with you again on _____.

Sincerely,

Steve Brennan

Subsection 8.1.j Letter #10, Follow-up to "Networking" Phone Call—Resume Enclosed

Ima Kneedy
1234 Any Street Drive NW
My City, WA 98335
222-XXX-XXXX
somebody@internet.com

Date

Decision Maker, Title
Company Name
Address
City, State Zip

Dear Name of Decision Maker:

I realize how little extra time you must have due to managing such a hectic schedule. However, your organization has truly piqued my curiosity, and I am convinced a meeting with you could prove mutually beneficial. Therefore, I am contacting you again in hopes that we would have an opportunity to meet at some point in the near future. Perhaps a number of considerations have prevented a positive response from you.

Regardless of our difficulty in connecting, my initial interest in your company has not diminished. I am firmly convinced my leadership and management expertise will enable me to be of immediate value to your firm.

Enclosed is a copy of my resume. If you will take this opportunity to read it, I think you will agree I have functional experience that would be well worth discussing.

Of course, a resume has its limitations and can only provide a brief overview of an individual's experience. Nevertheless, I hope you will be interested enough to provide me with an opportunity for a personal meeting. I will call you in the near future to set up an appointment to discuss mutual interests.

I look forward to speaking with you soon.

Sincerely,

Subsection 8.1.k Letter #11 Follow-up to "Networking" Phone Call—Resume Enclosed

Ima Kneedy
1234 Any Street Drive NW
My City, WA 98335
222-XXX-XXXX
somebody@internet.com

Date

Decision Maker, Title
Company Name
Address
City, State Zip

Dear Name of Decision Maker:

I really appreciate the time you spent with me on the phone the other day. As promised, I am enclosing my resume for you to examine. I hope it helps focus your thoughts regarding the questions I asked you over the phone.

Thank you for keeping my career search in mind. If you hear of any upcoming opportunities or think of someone I might contact, let me know.

Thanks again, and I will follow-up by phone in a few days.

Sincerely,

Subsection 8.1.1 Letter #12—Example Reply Letter

BOB ANYBODY
1234 Any Street Drive NW
My City, WA 98335
222-XXX-XXXX
somebody@internet.com

Date

Mr. Happy Face—Sr. Vice President
Mr. Direct Question—Regional Vice President
Blank Corporation

Dear Happy & Direct,

Thank you for the opportunity to visit your office yesterday and to be interviewed by at that time. The day was very informative and only intensified my desire to become your Seattle Location Manager.

I feel that my background and 25 years of business and sales management experience in a variety of disciplines serve me well in meeting the requirements of this challenging assignment.

I am convinced that my proven track record of increasing revenues and exemplary customer relations management (CRM) in each of my past environments coupled with my skill at creating positive change can provide both the immediate and long term results you desire.

I realize that your selection procedure requires that you gain consensus from everyone before you make your final selection. Accordingly, I will not expect to hear from you concerning my candidacy until you've completed your assessment

I look forward to hearing from you soon.

Sincerely,

Ms. Satisfied

➤ **Section 9.1** Interviewing Overview

Subsection 9.1.a General Interviewing Tips for candidates

Interviewing Tips for Candidates

Know the time and place of the interview and the interviewer's full name and title.

Ensure that you fully understand the job description of the position for which you are interviewing.

Plan to be 15 minutes early in anticipation of traffic problems or other unanticipated delays.

Also, know where you're going. If possible acquaint yourself with the route. Late arrival for a job interview is never excusable.

Dress professionally (i.e. proper business attire).

If presented with an application, fill it out neatly and completely.

Ensure to shake the interviewer's hand firmly.

Speak slowly and clearly. Don't rush your answers.

Stress accomplishments.

Ensure to answer every question fully and honestly.

Don't jump ahead or give more information than is required. Pay attention to "cutoff" cues.

Ensure you are consistent in your answers throughout all interviews.

Don't answer with a simple "yes" or "no". Explain answers where possible.

Avoid saying anything negative about present or previous employers or co-workers.

Ask questions to show interest in the Company and the position.

Ensure they know you are interested in the position; never close the door on an opportunity.

Look alert and interested at all times and look the interviewer in the eye.

Relax, smile and have a positive attitude. Give the appearance of energy as you walk.

WHAT TO PREPARE BEFOREHAND
(5 Step Process)

I) Chronological Outline of Career and Education

Break down your life into "segments" (i.e. university, first job, second job, etc.). For each segment, write down:

A.) why you went into the program or job;
B.) what you did when you were there; and
C.) why you left.

The chronology should flow logically and bring you to the present day. You should then write down where you want to be in the short and long term and why it makes sense based on where you've been according to your chronology. Also, write down the reasons why you would be appropriate for the job you are interviewing for and why you are interested in the position.

II) Strengths and Weaknesses

Strengths: Write down 3 technical and 3 non-technical personal strengths. For each strength, document something external that proves the strength is also perceived by others as strength, i.e. you received a bonus in recognition, there were some savings achieved, you completed the implementation of a system, you met objectives, it was noted on your performance evaluation.

Weaknesses: The area of weaknesses is difficult. The way to answer any question about your weaknesses is to either:

A.) describe a weakness or area for development that you have worked on and have now overcome; or

B.) describe a characteristic that could be perceived as either strength or a weakness.

III) <u>Questions to Ask</u>

It's important to ask a lot of questions both throughout the interview and at the end of the interview when interviewers generally ask if you have any questions. Therefore, you should prepare a list of 5-10 technical and 5-10 non-technical questions and memorize them before the interview. Do not inquire about salary, vacation, bonuses, or other benefits. This information should be discussed with your recruiter

Sample Questions:

1. Could you tell me about the growth plans and goals for the company/ department/ division?
2. What needs to be accomplished in this position in the next 6-12 months?
3. What skills are important to be successful in this position?
4. Why did you join this company?
5. What types of systems do you use throughout the company/department/ division?
6. Why is the position available?
7. What made the previous persons in this position successful/unsuccessful?
8. To where have successful people in this position advanced?
9. What criteria will my supervisor use for my performance evaluation and how frequently, and in what manner, will my supervisor and I meet?
10. How do you (the supervisor) like to operate in terms of assignments, delegation of responsibility and authority, general operating style, etc.?
11. What long and short term problems and opportunities do you think my prospective area faces?
12. With whom will I be interacting most frequently and what are their responsibilities and the nature of our interaction?
13. What particular things about my background, experience and style interest you?
14. What experience, training, attributes, operating style, accomplishments and personality factors should the "ideal" candidate for the job have?
15. Is there anything in my background or experience to prevent you from considering me as a viable candidate?
16. What else can I do to get a job offer from your company?
17. What is the time frame for making a decision on this position?

IV) <u>Questions You Should Be Prepared For</u>

1. What do you know about our company?
2. Why do you want to work here?
3. Why are you looking to change positions?
4. What are your strengths and weaknesses?
5. What do like most and least about your current position (or supervisor)?
6. Where do you see yourself in 5 years?
7. What are the best and worst things your boss would say about you?
8. Name 5 adjectives that would best describe you.
9. What are your concerns in your current situation and what would you improve?
10. How have you changed or improved the nature of your job?
11. Why should we hire you?
12. What can you do for us that someone else can't?
13. Why did you choose this particular vocation?
14. What contributions to profits have you made in your present or former positions to justify your salary level there?
15. What do you think determines a person's progress in a good company?

Source: S Brennan/Internet web-Google *job search*

Subsection 9.1.b Phone interview tips

Employers use <u>telephone interviews</u> as a way of identifying and recruiting candidates for employment. Phone interviews are often used to screen candidates in order to narrow the pool of applicants who will be invited for in-person interviews. They are also used as a way to minimize the expenses involved in interviewing out-of-town candidates.

While you're actively job searching, it's important to be prepared for a phone interview on a moment's notice. You never know when a recruiter or a networking contact might call and ask if you have a few minutes to talk.

Be Prepared to Interview

Prepare for a phone interview just as you would for a regular interview. Compile a list of your strengths and weaknesses, as well as a list of answers to typical <u>phone interview questions.</u> In addition, plan on being prepared for a phone conversation about your background and skills.

Keep your <u>resume</u> in clear view, on the top of your desk, or tape it to the wall near the phone, so it's at your fingertips when you need to answer questions.

Have a short list of your accomplishments available to review.

Have a pen and paper handy for note taking.

Turn call-waiting off so your call isn't interrupted.

If the time isn't convenient, ask if you could talk at another time and suggest some alternatives.

Clear the room—evict the kids and the pets. Turn off the stereo and the TV. Close the door.

Unless you're sure your cell phone service is going to be perfect, consider using a landline rather than your cell phone to avoid a dropped call or static on the line.

Practice Interviewing

Talking on the phone isn't as easy as it seems. I've always found it's helpful to practice. Have a friend or family member conduct a <u>mock interview</u> and tape record it so you can see how you sound over the phone. Any cassette recorder will work. You'll be able to hear your "ums" and "us" and "okay's" and you can practice reducing them from your conversational speech. Also rehearse answers to those typical questions you'll be asked.

During the Phone Interview

Don't smoke, chew gum, eat, or drink.

Do keep a glass of water handy, in case you need to wet your mouth.

Smile. Smiling will project a positive image to the listener and will change the tone of your voice.

Speak slowly and enunciate clearly.

Use the person's title (Mr. or Ms. and their last name.) Only use a first name if they ask you to.

Don't interrupt the interviewer.

Take your time—it's perfectly acceptable to take a moment or two to collect your thoughts.

Give short answers.

Remember your goal is to set up a face-to-face interview. After you thank the interviewer ask if it would be possible to meet in person.

Source: S. Brennan/Internet web/tools Google job search

Subsection 9.1.c Sample questions for candidate to ask employer

1. Have you considered internal candidates for this position?
2. Mr. ___ What are you trying to accomplish with this position?
3. What in my career history sparked your interest?
4. What gave rise to the need for this position?
5. What do you expect from the successful candidate in the first 90 days?
6. What do you personally like about working at this company?"
7. Who currently performs these functions?
8. To whom will I report?
9. Where does this position fit into the organization?
10. What are the supervisory, managerial, and leadership responsibilities of the position?
11. What type of qualities would your ideal candidate bring to the position & to your organization?
12. Why is this position so critical to the company's immediate & long-term success?
13. What is the greatest challenge the region & or company faces today?
14. Tell me about advancement & promotional opportunities?

Subsection 9.1.d Sample behavioral questions asked by employer

1. Give an example of an occasion when you used logic to solve a problem.
2. Give an example of a goal you reached and tell me how you achieved it.
3. Give an example of a goal you didn't meet and how you handled it.
4. Describe a stressful situation at work and how you handled it.
5. Tell me about how you worked effectively under pressure.
6. How do you handle a challenge?

7. Have you been in a situation where you didn't have enough work to do?
8. Have you ever made a mistake? How did you handle it?
9. Describe a decision you made that was unpopular and how you handled implementing it.
10. Did you ever make a risky decision? Why? How did you handle it?
11. Did you ever postpone making a decision? Why?
12. Have you ever dealt with company policy you weren't in agreement with? How?
13. Have you gone above and beyond the call of duty? If so, how?
14. When you worked on multiple projects how did you prioritize them?
15. How did you handle meeting a tight deadline?
16. Give an example of how you set goals and achieve them.
17. Did you ever not meet your goals? Why?
18. What do you do when your schedule is interrupted? Give an example of how you handle it.
19. Have you had to convince a team to work on a project they weren't thrilled about? How did you do it?
20. Give an example of how you worked on team.
21. Have you handled a difficult situation with a co-worker? How?
22. What do you do if you disagree with a co-worker?
23. Share an example of how you were able to motivate employees or co-workers.
24. Do you listen? Give an example of when you did or when you didn't listen.
25. Have you handled a difficult situation with a supervisor? How?
26. Have you handled a difficult situation with another department? How?
27. Have you handled a difficult situation with a client or vendor? How?
28. What do you do if you disagree with your boss?

Source: S. Brennan/Internet web/tools Google job search

Subsection 9.1.e Example of How to Answer

Tell me a little about yourself

I'm a well-qualified Sr. level sales management, and marketing executive. I have continually been challenged to deliver results that required strong strategic sales leadership. I'm task oriented and result driven. In all of my prior positions I have delivered significant financial improvements in revenue, market share, and bottom line profitability, and I'm well respected within my industry.

On the personal side, I'm happily married with two children and 6 beautiful grandchildren. I consider myself active. I enjoy working out at the gym, cross country skiing, boating, water skiing, back packing, and golf. Additionally, I ride my motorcycle and play drums.

Subsection 9.1.f What do you consider your key career accomplishments?

Example of How to Answer

What do you consider your key career accomplishments?

There are few major achievements, which standout in my career. The first one that comes to mind is when I was given my first operation store management assignment with XXXXXXX. I was assigned to a store that had an 8-year history for losing money. In my first year as manager I was able to turn a modest profit of $19K and reduce the AR to 2.3% for 10% past due. My second success was with XXXXXX where the vice president and I negotiated the largest contract ever reported in the industry to date. The opening order was for $1.1 million tc XXXXX with continuing revenue of $25 million annually. At XXXXX I received the National Sales Fleet Manager on the year award for selling more national account fleet customers the all the other 50 representatives in the company.

And lastly at XXXXX my sales team & I finished up $1.7 million in revenue adding $700K in bottom line profit.

Subsection 9.1.g Why are you considering leaving your current position?

Example of How to Answer

Why are you considering leaving your current position?

Let me first say XXXXX is a very good organization and well-managed company. However, even though I have achieved a good deal of success, and have been steadily promoted too increasingly more responsible management positions during my tenure here. I originally set some goals for myself when I started. My main objective for employment at XXXXX was to work at one of the XXXXX this opening has not been afforded me. I am very excited for the opportunity to become part of the truck sales team at XXXXX.

Source S. Brennan

Subsection 9.1.h Top stress questions & answers

Here are some of the most commonly asked stress or interview questions and suggested approaches for answering them. Bear in mind that the two main issues on the interviewer's mind are...

- What can you do for me?
- Do you fit in?

Consequently, if you can use these questions as a means to make points on either of these issues, you'll gain an edge on your competition.

Tell me about yourself

Keep this answer focused either on the job at hand, or if this is an exploratory interview, on your qualifications.

This is not an invitation to take the interviewer on a long-winded tour through high school and college. For example, if you are being interviewed for a production management position, you might say,

> I have over 13 years of production experience. Starting as an Assistant Foreman, I was promoted to Foreman and then Plant Superintendent with the XYZ Company. When I moved on to the ABC Company, I gained additional experience in production and inventory control. In addition, I have 4 years of experience in your industry as well as a degree in Business Administration.

In short, your answer should be a quick overview of those parts of your professional background that are relevant to the job for which you are being interviewed. Try not to go on and on. One minute is about the outer limit.

If the interviewer asks you to take him or her on a tour of your career, start with today and work backward. Hit the highlights and don't get bogged down in irrelevant detail.

What are your Short Range objectives?

The key, once again, is to keep your answer focused on the job for which you are interviewing. It is not in your best interest to pick short-range objectives that the job or company might be unable to provide.

For example, if you are being interviewed by a newly appointed sales manager who is in his mid-thirties, your objective should not be, *"I want to be a sales manager in no more than 18 months."* That will probably scare off the interviewer. Even if it doesn't, it sets you up as a high probability for turnover.

What are your long term objectives?

In dealing with this question, it is a good idea to remain flexible. A brief answer that refers to moving up the ladder as quickly and as far as your capabilities permit will suffice.

You have an opportunity to turn the question around. For example, you might say, "My long-range objectives are somewhat flexible and would depend, of course, upon the opportunities and strategic direction of the company. I would appreciate your view on what opportunities there might be down the road."

What do you look for in a job?

As in the answer about short-range objectives, bias your answer toward the job for which you are being interviewed.

Be prepared to answer questions about the type of working environment you are seeking. Here again, stay somewhat general and flexible. For example, you might say, "While I am a team player, I also look for the opportunity to exercise some independence in carrying out the duties of my position."

Why are you leaving?

As with many other of these questions, there is no single right answer. As a general guideline, focus on the positive. Don't tarnish your professional image by casting aspersions on your past or present companies or on your past or present bosses. In addition, do not share confidential or proprietary information.

Good reasons to be leaving (looking for a job) include…

- Company's growth has not been as fast as expected and promotional opportunities are severely limited.
- You have outgrown the position and your further progress is blocked.
- Despite your best efforts, the business is not doing well. In short, someone else dropped the ball.
- The company is moving to a geographic area that you don't find attractive.

What can you do for us that someone else cannot do?

It's hard for you to say what someone else can do, so focus on yourself and your capabilities. Your answer might go something like this.

> *Mr. Interviewer, I do not know who else you may have talked to so that it would be somewhat inappropriate for me to comment. What I can comment on, however, are my qualifications which include _____, _____, and _____. How do you see those types of qualifications fitting in here?*

Why should we hire you?

There are two ways to deal with a question...

- Answer it—Respond to it.

This type of question may give an opportunity to give a response rather than an answer. For example, if you have approached a company cold and have been invited in on very short notice, you probably do not have a very good answer to this question.

Instead, focus your response on why you wrote to the company. It might go something like this.

> *Well, Mr. Interviewer, I wrote to your company because it would seem that there is a good match between what I have to offer and what your company might need. Let me ask you what it was about my background that caught your attention?*

How good is your health?

This question may be the age liability in sheep's clothing. In addition, the interviewer may be concerned because your projection is that of a person who is not in particularly good health or one who lacks a high energy level.

The obvious answer is your health is fine. You should go on to state that you are accustomed to working long hours and are quite capable of keeping up a fast pace.

If you have a specific health problem that the interviewer may know about or could easily find out about, then you must give a truthful answer. However, you should go on to point out that your condition has had no adverse effect on performance, attendance or ability to give 100%.

Can you work under pressure, deadlines, etc.?

This question is an invitation for you to not only say yes, but to support your claim with an example. Cite an episode in which you worked under great pressure or had to meet a deadline that was close at hand. The competitive edge lies in giving an example where other candidates probably will not.

What is your philosophy of management?

The danger inherent in this question is simple. You don't know the interviewer's philosophy. If you adopt a hard stance, one of two things will happen: you will either become a stellar candidate or you will have terminated your candidacy.

Instead, preface your answer with a statement that shows flexibility. For example, you might say,

> *Given the kinds of jobs that I have had and the kinds of people that I have inherited, what I have found to be effective is* _____
> _____."

By giving such an answer, you have demonstrated that you are adaptable and can change your philosophy to fit the situation at hand.

If the interviewer is sharp, he may ask you why you have adopted this particular philosophy. There are a number of themes around which you can build your answer. Some are...

- You have seen such a philosophy work in the past or you have seen other approaches fail.
- Your gut feeling is that such a philosophy should work.
- It is compatible with your general operating style and overall philosophy.

Do you prefer line or staff work? Why?

If the job for which you are interviewing is a staff job, we strongly recommend that you prefer staff work, at least for the sake of this interview. The same holds true for a line position. When answering the question, "Why?" a few examples are listed below.

> *I prefer staff work because it has enabled me to become an expert in the field of my choice and has also enabled me to use that expertise to contribute to the general management process.*

> *I prefer line work because the line is really where it happens. On the line, you get to implement your thoughts and actions, and see the results quickly.*

> *That is a difficult question. As a Staff Manager in Personnel, I obviously like staff work. However, my job has elements of a line job as well. My line organization, the Personnel Department, provides service to the rest of the organization…staff expertise. So, staff work gives me the best of both possible worlds, in that it has both line and staff functions.*

What are your biggest accomplishments in your present or last job?

In citing your accomplishments, pick those that seem to line up well with the major elements of the position under consideration. For example, if you have accomplishments in both cost and general accounting, and you are interviewing for a general accounting position, bias your answer toward general accounting accomplishments.

Your goal is to show the interviewer that your accomplishments line up with his needs.

What is your biggest strength?

Pick strengths that are relevant to the position at hand. For example, if the job for which you are being interviewed seems to require someone who is detail oriented, then one of your strengths should be strong orientation to detail.

What is your biggest weakness?

We all have them. Choose one that's either irrelevant to the job for which you're being considered or one that is really too much of a good thing.

For example, a candidate for a sales position might say,

I don't like to lose and there are times I'd be better off moving on to a new prospect than spending additional time trying to sell someone who is unlikely to buy. I've gotten better at this, but I don't think I'll ever be able to accept losing all that gracefully.

How long would it take you to make a contribution to our firm?

This question may be the interviewer's way of saying he is concerned about your lack of experience in his industry. Indicate that you are confident of your ability to contribute rapidly and support your claim with an example.

How long would you stay with us?

This may be the interviewer's way of saying he thinks you might be a job-hopper. However, a response which attempts to illustrate your commitment by indicating that you will stay with XYZ Company until they carry you out in a box has little credibility.

A more productive response might go something like,

Mr. Jones, in my next position, I want two things: an environment that will challenge me and an organization within which I will be recognized for my contributions. As long as those two elements exist, I would probably have no

Mr. Jones, I have always prided myself on my high degree of professionalism. One thing that means to me is that I evaluate people within the work place based only upon their performance. I make every effort to be fair with those I work with no matter what their background or personal preferences.

Other useful options include providing a non-answer answer such as, *"My views on abortion are not abnormal"* or simply taking a neutral stance and arguing both sides of the issue.

If you could start again, what would you do differently?

Remembering that liabilities exist only if perceived, don't allow the interviewer to give you a nice length of rope with which to hang yourself.

Honesty in response to a question like this (i.e. I would have gone on to get my MBA; I wouldn't have stayed with XYZ Company as long as I did; I never would have gone into engineering) will not gain you "points" for honesty, but will tarnish the interviewer's perception of your background.

Therefore, keep your response short and credible. Say something like,

> *Well, Mr. Jones, obviously with 20-20 hindsight, any one of us would probably make some changes if they could. However, on the whole I would have to say that I am extremely proud of my achievements and quite happy with my career progression to date.*

How do you rate yourself as a professional? As an executive?

A good way to handle a question like this is to introduce an objective yardstick against which you will compare yourself.

In other words, an answer might be

> *Well, Ms. Interviewer, if a criterion for a top-notch sales executive is the ability to generate new business while maximizing the productivity of national accounts, I would have to rate myself as top-notch. My reasons are simple. Over the course of my tenure with Stentz Systems, I have _____ _____."*

What do you think of your boss?

Obviously, if you think your boss is great, then it is pretty easy to answer this question.

On the other hand, if a part of your reason for leaving your last position was the fact that you really didn't get along with your boss, then responding to this question becomes challenging.

Avoid issues of personality or politics. While you may be very well justified in your view of your boss as someone less than a paradigm of management excellence, the interview is not the place to discuss his or her shortcomings. Doing so will make you sound like a whiner or troublemaker.

Instead, comment briefly on some positive aspects of your boss, be they in his personality or her management style...and leave it at that.

Why haven't you obtained a job so far?

If you've been on the market for a while, then the interviewer may conclude that if no one else will hire you, he shouldn't either. Being apologetic or simply saying that it's a tough market in your field will not help either.

Depending upon the length of your unemployment, it may be enough to respond that you are not seeking a job, but rather are looking for the right career opportunity and have not yet found the environment within which you want to commit your time and energies.

If your unemployment has been at all lengthy, then it will be very useful for you to develop a "game plan" as to why you have been "on the beach" for so long. In other words, if you can appear to have been purposeful and directed during this period, you can overcome the interviewer's possible conjecture that nobody else has wanted to hire you.

You can also mention any consulting work you've done, even if you weren't paid for it.

What features of your previous job have you disliked?

It's unlikely that you'll be believed if you say that you loved everything about your previous positions. Therefore, be prepared in advance with several "moderate annoyances" that you can relate. But make sure that these annoyances are unlikely to be part of the interviewer's company's environment. For example, if you are interviewing with General Motors, this would not be a good time to relate that you don't like working for big companies.

Would you describe a few situations in which your work was criticized?

In responding to this question, you have two options:

Be prepared with an episode of a "lesson learned" from earlier in your career. Relate an incident in which you were criticized, recognized your mistake, and learned from that situation. A good way to begin your response is to emphasize the words, *"Earlier in my career, _____."*

Pick a weakness that is really "a little too much of a good thing." See the answer to "What's your biggest weakness for further guidance.

How would you evaluate your present firm?

The object here is to avoid criticizing the firm or its people.

Don't say bad things about your present company. Even if they are true, the interviewer probably knows neither you nor your firm and is apt to perceive you as a whiner.

Remember also, this answer should be compatible with the interviewer's possible question, "Why do you want to leave your present company?"

Do you generally speak to people before they speak to you?

Obviously, your answer cannot be either a blanket yes or a blanket no. It depends on the situation.

You might say something like,

> *Well, that depends entirely on the situation. However, if you are asking that question to determine my general operating style, let me assure you that I am an outgoing, gregarious person who has no trouble meeting and building rapport with new people.*

What was the last book you read, movie you saw, and sporting event you attended?

These questions provide information from which an interviewer can draw conclusions about your personality and interests. Unless the movie or book is controversial, tell the truth. But it's important that you have read, seen, or attended whatever you claimed since more detailed questioning may follow.

What interests you most about the position we have? The least?

The response to the former should be an aspect or aspects of the job that benefit the employer not you. For example, you might cite the challenge of the problems to be solved, or the opportunity to apply your well-honed skills to particular tasks that need doing.

The answer to the latter question should equivocate, i.e., "At this point I have not heard of anything about the job that turns me off."

Don't you feel you might be better off in a different size company? Different type of company?

Either one these questions is probably a liability coming at you on a tangent. For example, questions about your being better off in a different type company are probably the "No experience in the prospective employer's industry" liability coming at you on the oblique.

Relate a situation in which you were thrust into a new situation where you learned and contributed quickly.

Questions about a different size company could mean that the prospective employer perceives a mismatch between the size of his company and the size of the companies in which you gained your experience.

If you are being interviewed by a small company and your background is in large companies, relate that even a large company is composed of smaller elements and that the organization within the large company for which you worked operated quite autonomously. Draw parallels and point out similarities where they exist.

Why aren't you earning more at your age?

The interviewer may equate your low earnings with low value.

If you are in a low paying industry, make sure that you point out that you have received raises that are indicative of superior performance. Also point out that your industry/function is traditionally low paying, which is one of the reasons you are looking for a new job.

When discussing how much you are making, try to respond in terms of value of the job. For example, you might say,

> *My position has a range that goes from $45,000 to $75,000 and I am well over the midpoint. In fact, in recognition of my performance, I am one of the best paid in the company.*

The objective in dealing with this question is to show that your perceived low pay does not equate to low value or poor performance.

Will you be out to take your boss's job?

If you say simply yes, the interviewer may wonder what lengths you will go to in order to get your boss's job. If you simply say no, then the interviewer will wonder if you have any ambition at all.

This question can be much more easily dealt with if you modify it somewhat before answering. For example, you might say,

> *Well, if I had the opportunity to get ahead, that certainly would be a plus. Of course, I would welcome the opportunity to get my boss's job. However, the*

way I see that happening is by my working as hard as I possibly can at the job that I have. By doing so, I would hope that my talents become recognized and that I will be considered promotable to my boss's job and to other jobs that may come open too.

I do want you to understand that I am a team player and that the promotions that I have had in the past have been won primarily by my working in support of my boss's objectives as best I can.

Are you adaptable, creative, and analytical, a good manager, a leader, etc.?

To simply answer, "Yes," is insufficient. You've done nothing to grab a competitive edge. Everybody else who is asked these questions is also answering, "Yes."

You can stand out from the crowd by giving an example to support your claim. For example, you may be asked whether you are adaptable. Your answer might go something like this:

Yes, I am adaptable. For example, when I joined the XYZ Company as Sales Manager, I had never worked with products like XYZ's before, so I had a lot to learn. Yet, it was my job to put together a nationwide sales force as quickly as possible.

At first, I poured over all the technical publications and other manuals I could get my hands on. I also asked lots of questions of the people in research and development as well as those in production.

Make a long story short, even though the product was new to me, I put together a sales team that within 6 months increased sales by 50%. I also personally signed up a few major accounts including one my boss had been trying to land for more than a year. Is that the kind of adaptability you meant?"

By claiming a qualification and then validating it with an example, you will make your candidacy much more credible and memorable to the interviewer.

How would you describe your own personality?

There is no "right" answer to this question. Mention attributes that are important to be successful for the position under consideration. You can avoid sounding too self-serving by beginning your answer with a phrase like,

Others have said that I am _____, _____ and _____.

Have you helped increase sales? Profits? Reduce costs?

Don't forget that when all is said and done, a large portion of any interviewer's heart lives at the bottom line. While things like motivation, leadership qualities, and managerial skills are important, ultimately (in one way or another) you will be hired based upon your ability to enhance the bottom line. For that reason, you should have specific examples.

This is an opportunity for you to sell yourself through the vehicle of another's viewpoint.

What do your subordinates think of you?

Offer strengths and attributes that are relevant to your ability to perform well in the position for which you're being considered.

Have you fired people before?

This question gives you an opportunity to show that you are both tough and compassionate. If you have fired someone, say something like,

> *I think anyone who has been in management for any length of time has been in a position where they have had to terminate someone. While it is never easy and certainly must be done in the proper manner, it is often best for both the individual and organization. In my view, human resources represent a major cost factor, and substandard performance cannot be ignored."*

If the answer is no, do your best to substantiate that you have had substantial input into the performance appraisal and disciplinary procedures within your area. You can also point out that you were able to bring substandard employees up to speed and that you then had no need to fire them.

Have you hired people before? What do you look for?

What is important here is to know your own mind prior to the interview.

If you have hired people for different functions, you might look for different things for each function. For example, you might look for assertiveness in sales people and detail-orientation in people being considered for general accounting positions.

Why do you want to work for us?

The answer here is similar to the question, "Why should we hire you?"

If this question is asked very early in the interview, you may not really have a good answer. Therefore, give a response instead. Here is an example.

> *Based on what I learned about your organization from people I know, I did some research and found that you have achieved impressive sales increases for the last 6 consecutive quarters. Given that kind of growth, I felt that my strong background in _____ and _____ might be valuable to you. For my part, I have worked for both growing and contracting companies, and growing companies are a lot more fun and a lot more challenging.*

If you had your choice of jobs and companies, where would you go?

In answering the part of this question about jobs, simply relate that you are looking at other positions or situations similar to the job for which you are being interviewed. You are trying to give the interviewer an impression of someone who is focused.

Regarding companies, don't mention the specific names of other companies you may be considering unless the interviewer really presses hard. The interviewer might conclude that his company is your second or third choice, which does nothing to help your candidacy.

Instead, focus on job content and company situation. For example, you might say,

> *What I am looking for is not a specific company, but the right situation. To me, the right situation is a company that has a position that is challenging and where the prospects for the future are good. The way I see it, the best way for me to get ahead is to help a company succeed.*

Why do you feel you have top management potential?

If you have served in top management positions, simply state that it is not really a question of potential but a question of where your well-developed skills and abilities would be most applicable. Cite examples of positions (titles notwithstanding) where you have had overall management responsibility.

For example, even the most humble manager of a small, three-person loan company may be functioning as a top manager if "corporate" allows him to operate autonomously.

If you have truly not had any top management experience, cite your ability to see the big picture as well as your awareness of how the jobs you've held have influenced the bottom line. Stress your profit orientation.

Source: S. Brennan/Internet tools

Subsection 9.1.i YouTube Interview(s)

These videos provide an important insight on listening, & answering questions

Copy these and insert into your browser

Introduction
http://www.youtube.com/watch?v=ns4Ks4EavwE

Types of Interviews
http://www.youtube.com/watch?v=-KEYe3gO68k

Research the Company
http://www.youtube.com/watch?v=lEue6UgLrO8

Typical Questions
http://www.youtube.com/watch?v=wU_6l4iyFYc

Behavioral Questions
http://www.youtube.com/watch?v=WgMKLoOXXCY

Practice
http://www.youtube.com/watch?v=8lO6OzOzshY

Day of Interview Preparation
http://www.youtube.com/watch?v=KphWK4dThlQ

Interview Introduction
http://www.youtube.com/watch?v=Jai6o6ABt0

Non-Verbal's
http://www.youtube.com/watch?v=Y_zNIjSd-7k

Questions to Ask—Not to Ask
http://www.youtube.com/watch?v=6hWW4EReLW8

Close of the Interview
http://www.youtube.com/watch?v=1Wd8GptIjoM

Thank You Notes
http://www.youtube.com/watch?v=rXoD8wjFHM4

Summary
http://www.youtube.com/watch?v=dYWMZUysXrU

Source: Previously posted—http://www.Youtube.com The Employment net Work

➤ Section 10.0 Finishing Touches

Subsection 10.1.a Dress for Success

Once you've landed that interview there are a few specifics that everyone should do to be ready.

Review

Review what you've learned about the prospective employer. Re-read the trade journals, research the internet, and find articles about them. If they are a publically traded company see what their stock value is. Have they been growing? What are their plans for future growth? Is their business growing or contracting? Sometime during the interview just mentioning a small statistic or fun factoid is very beneficial. It lets them know you took time to understand a little about them.

Plan your wardrobe

Men—Both a dark blue or grey suit, or sport coat with dress slacks, new shirt, and a complementary tie along with a pair of dark shined shoes is best.

I mentored a young man who was in the trades as a Master Electrician. I advised him to wear a new shirt, non-obtrusive tie, and a sport coat, along with shined shoes and to take it easy on the cologne. However, there could be exceptions as in the case of the automotive industry, where over dressing is not advised. In this case a nice pair of khakis, pressed button down shirt, and shined shoes may be more appropriate.

Women—Same for you too, a dark blue suit or grey skirt works best. The length of the either should be a little below the knee line. Blouses should not be low cut and should be made of cotton or silk in a neutral color, preferably white another other light color. Please go easy on makeup, and as with men, light on the perfume. You should wear conservative lipstick and nail polish, and be sure your panty hose do not have any runs.

Subsection 10.1.b Positive Self Talk

It is very important that you are confident, convinced, with a positive attitude feeding your mind, and knowing you're an excellent candidate. Even after 47 years of business, personal, and economic, and journey, I still begin everyday feeding myself with positive affirmations.

Below are just couple of the exercises I did in the beginning to reshape my thinking, which may help you as well. First get some 3X5 index cards. At the top the first one write:

I AM—followed by:

I AM—Honest, Responsible, Motivated, Cheerful, Flexible, Enthusiastic, Loyal, Faithful, Capable, I have a Positive Mental Attitude.

I AM Wonderfully Made. There is No One like Me!

I have terrific transferrable skills, and my new perfect assignment is being created for me right now!

I expect the best every day. All things work great for me today. This is a new and wonderful day for me. No obstacle, difficulty, or delay will be an issue, all good things come to me as I am blessed.

I am a mental magnet attracting to myself all things which bless and prosper me. I am going to enjoy excellent success in everything I do today.

I provide outstanding service and everyone I come in contact with are blessed by what I have to offer. I give my talents freely, and all my work and efforts come to full fruition.

Please read these positive affirmations daily, and speak them out loud. Add others that will reflect your desires. If we don't first believe good things about ourselves who will?

Next, close your eyes, breath slowly, allow yourself to relax, and then visualize yourself in the profession you want, and say quietly to yourself, "I'm proud to be the Project Manager (or whatever your desired career specialty may be) at XYZ Corporation."

Sometimes we may not attain the position at the company we visualized. This should not dissuade you from continuing to read your daily affirmations or using your visualization techniques.

I'm a huge proponent of picturing in one's mind's eye. However, it was still very hard for me when I did not make the cut on an interview, but I just said to myself, "God has me in His Hand." Every effort that you make increases your odds of landing your dream assignment.

Subsection 10.1.c 24 hours before your big day

Always double check to know exactly where you are going. Whether your interview is local or out of town, drive by it to make sure you know exactly where the company is located.

If out of town, drive the night before from your hotel, ask the hotel manager how traffic is 1 hour before your scheduled interview time. This will give you plenty of time to arrive.

Be sure your attire is good to go, no wrinkles or issues. You want to look your best. Make sure you have you have a few copies of your resume in case someone asks for it. Have your interview questions typed and prepared in the order you want to ask them.

Remember to always be yourself, relax, use some of your positive self-talk, and ***"Walk in Quiet Confidence."***

Because each of you made the commitment to purchase my book, and have done the work as outlined in it, I have an offer for you. I'll provide each of you with some personal feedback.

You may email me up to 3 questions regarding anything to do with your individual employment situation. If you're interested in individual coaching, please email me for information.

Contact Information:

Steve Brennan
yourmentor@outlook.com

Or visit
www.meaningfulemployment.com